KT-549-360

The Schooling and Identity
of Asian Girls

The Schooling and Identity of Asian Girls

Farzana Shain

Trentham Books

Stoke on Trent, UK and Sterling, USA

Trentham Books Limited

Westview House	22883 Quicksilver Drive
734 London Road	Sterling
Oakhill	VA 20166-2012
Stoke on Trent	USA
Staffordshire	
England ST4 5NP	

First published 2003

British Library Cataloguing-in-Publication Data
A catalogue record for this book is available from the British Library

1 85856 181 7

Cover photography by Farzana Shain

Designed and typeset by Trentham Print Design Ltd., Chester and printed in Great Britain by Cromwell Press Ltd., Wiltshire.

Contents

For Aky – (Mirza Akhter)
Love and respect – always.

Acknowledgements

I wish to thank the students and staff in the research schools who gave up valuable time to speak to me. I am extremely grateful to Jenny Ozga and to Ken Jones for their support and also for commenting on earlier drafts of chapters – any remaining errors are, of course, my own. Thanks are also due to Joe Sim for years of solid support.

I am particularly indebted to Gillian Klein at Trentham for her consistent support, encouragement and above all patience, during the final year of this project. Thanks are also due to Jan Peterson, Mike Johnson and Tim Brighouse for valuable advice and assistance in the early stages of the research project.

I wish to acknowledge the support of others – family and friends – who helped me in various ways when needed: Pannu Khan, Raqia Begum, Ash, Shani, Assie, Aky, Seb Navaranjan, Richard Wild, Nafsika Alexiadou, Siadjana Ivanis, David Pye and Azrini Wahidin; but, most of all, Bülent Gökay without whose support this book would never have been finished.

Introduction

In the summer of 2001, disturbances broke out across towns and cities in England involving Asian[1] and white youth in clashes with the police. The first occurred in Bradford at Easter but during the late spring and early summer spread to other towns: Oldham (26th – 28th May), Leeds (5 June) Burnley (23rd–24th June), Bradford (7 July), Stoke-on-Trent (14 July) – earning them the label of 'racial hotspots' (Harris, 2001). The disturbances in Oldham, where police in riot-gear battled with over 500 men for control of the streets in the mainly Asian Glodwick area for three nights at the end of May, were described as the 'worst riots in Britain for 15 years' (Carter, 2001). The false accusation that Asians gangs had created no-go areas for whites in Oldham cast them as the perpetrators of crime rather than the victims of racism and racial harassment.

While various explanations were offered in public and private debates – many pointing to racism, deprivation and high unemployment in the northern towns and cities, the Cantle report (Home Office, 2001), the official enquiry into the causes of the 'riots', suggested the main explanatory factor was self-segregation. It was argued that although physical segregation is nothing new, the fact that white people's and black people's lives barely touch each other is a cause for concern. The strategy advanced in the report is *community cohesion*. Translated into practice this means the twinning of schools, the encouragement of dialogue between youth supported by a community cohesion taskforce and promoting the merging of different communities. In themselves these recommendations are neither spectacular nor problematic. But when the political context is taken into consideration – that the report was commissioned to investigate what had been the *causes* of the disturbances – the recommendations become quite alarming. The implication is that racism is *caused* by segregation rather than *causing* it. The picture that emerges is of racism as being caused by the failure of particular groups to integrate.

The publication of the report in the aftermath of September 11 2001 – the attack on America in which two hijacked planes were deliberately crashed into the World Trade Centre in New York – and the ensuing 'war on terrorism' was significant in focusing the spotlight firmly on Muslim communities and their cultural practices. The 'war on terrorism' has largely been justified with assertions of the barbarity of Islam and its threat to the world order. The demonising of Muslim communities across the globe has meant that the word Muslim has become synony-mous with terror and evil and that anyone of 'Muslim' appearance (generally anyone from the middle-east or the subcontinent) can be treated with suspicion, hostility, detained under new anti-terrorism laws or attacked – as several of the revenge attacks for September 11 bear out. Issues of freedom and control have once again placed women at the centre of debate – as the markers of cultural boundaries – with the *hijab* coming to symbolise ultimate control and restriction of women by men.

Following the publication of the Cantle report in December 2001, Home Secretary David Blunkett also drew on arguments about religious and cultural practices in his pronouncements on religion and integration. In part this was to support new proposed legislation on terrorism and on asylum. Blunkett announced, for example, that the government was considering an oath of allegiance for immigrants (to the British state and British norms) and that English language tests would be introduced. He argued that practices such as forced marriages and genital mutilation had been allowed to continue because of an over-emphasis on cultural difference and 'moral relativism'. In May 2002 he also talked about introducing segregated schooling (though this has been widely rejected) for the children of asylum seekers.

What emerges from Blunkett's proclamations is an image of an isolated Asian (mainly Muslim) community that clings to backward practices, does not bother to learn the English language and does not want to integrate into mainstream society. The family and elders once com-mended for transmitting to youngsters the strong values of discipline and hard work are now charged with either holding them back or corrupting them: mothers by not learning the language, families for not allowing or enabling them to adopt the values of the mainstream, and religious leaders of promoting dangerous ideas. Asian boys and young men once characterised as passive and hardworking are now repositioned as aggressive, volatile and hot-headed – in short as a threat to the social order. This shift in representation from the passive and hardworking Asian boy to the fundamentalist has been underway for some time – since the late 1980s and early 1990s and particularly in the wake of events such as the Rushdie affair and the Gulf War, discussed in the next chapter. The themes of freedom and control, integration and isolation that emerge from the events outlined are central to current representations of Asian girls as the over-controlled victims of oppressive cultures. Current discourses on Asian masculinity in particular are central to the positioning of Asian girls as passive, timid and shy. Since masculinity is defined in relation to femininity – it is what femininity is not – the more aggressive, dangerous and volatile Asian boys and men appear to be, the more passive, controlled and vulnerable Asian girls are assumed to be.

In this book I set out to challenge these misconceptions of Asian girls by presenting a set of alternative accounts directly from Asian girls themselves. These accounts reveal that rather than being the passive victims of oppressive cultures, the girls are actively engaged in producing identities that draw on both residual cultures of the home and the local and regional cultures they now inhabit. The empirical research on which this book draws was conducted for my doctoral thesis. Through a detailed analysis of the accounts of forty four young working class women of Pakistani, Bangladeshi and Indian descent, I explore a range of Asian femininities as they are managed and performed in the context of schooling. A total of eight secondary schools across Greater Manchester and Staffordshire were the main sites for the research.

The book is essentially about the ways in which Asian girls make sense of schooling. However, rather than focusing purely on the micro level of classroom interaction, my approach places emphasis on schools as sites where wider relations of power are both reinforced and challenged. I am particularly interested in the way that wider discourses on gender, race, class and age, as they are filtered through popular constructions of Asian femininity, impact on the girls' identities, by which I mean struggles over modes of 'being'. I agree with Brah that 'identity is never a fixed core, but on the other hand changing identities do assume specific concrete patterns as in a kaleidoscope against particular sets of historical and social circumstances' (1992: 142-3).

In the chapters that follow, I outline in more detail my approach to understanding issues of schooling and identity against the backdrop of such historical and social circumstances. In the next chapter, I refer briefly to my conceptualisation of racism in order to explore some dominant media representations that impact on the schooling and identity of Asian girls. The media continues to play a powerful role in shaping commonsense assumptions about Asian groups that can lead to or produce 'real' or material effects at the levels of schooling and society. That is, I am concerned to explore some current media *discourses* on Asian femininity.

Following Mulhern (2000) I take the term discourse to mean

> ..language in action. In its strong, contemporary sense...it asserts the priority of socially formed practices of language over the action of individuals who necessarily operate in and through them. A discourse is more or less systematic sets of forms, topics and procedures that regulate both the object of utterance – what is 'seen' and spoken of – and its subjects – the identities that we assume, consciously or not, in practising it (Mulhern, 2000: 181)[2]

The book reveals how wider discourses on Asian femininity impact on the girls' experiences of schooling in terms of both the ways in which they are positioned and how they position themselves in relation to these discourses. Central to these positionings is the concept of racism.

My focus is on how wider discourses of Asian femininity impact on the girls' experiences of schooling in terms of the ways in which they are positioned and how they position themselves in relation to these discourses. Central to these feminine discourses are current conceptions of Asian boys as a threat to the social order. In the second part of chapter One, I explore some of the events that were critical in shaping these current discourses on Asian youth, especially boys and young men, and locate this analysis in the broader context of a 'racialisation of Britishness'.

In chapters two and three, I set the context for the empirical research that I present in later chapters. In chapter two, I outline the theoretical framework that underpins the book and in chapter three I explore the concept of resistance as it has been employed in the youth literature and specifically in the literature on Asian girls. In chapters four to seven I outline and discuss four of the strategies that Asian girls in the research employed to deal with their everyday experiences in the context of schooling. In the final chapter I draw out some conclusions and explore some practical issues with regard to the schooling of Asian girls.

Notes

1 Throughout the book, the term *Asian* is employed to refer to people who have, or whose parents or grandparents have, migrated from the Indian subcontinent (including via Africa) to Britain. The term *black* is used in its political sense and therefore includes both those of African Caribbean and South Asian origin.

2 I am extremely grateful to Ken Jones for pointing me to this definition.

1

New racisms, old pathologies

There is not the space here to engage in a full discussion of the concept of racism. Broadly speaking, racism refers to a set of beliefs, attitudes and practices whose outcome, whether intentional or unintentional, results in discrimination against particular groups on the grounds of colour, culture, ethnicity, nationality or religion. However, the concept of racism on which I draw emphasises its socially and historically variable character. As Hall (1981) argued in his pioneering essay, racism is not a unitary phenomenon but is concretely articulated with other forms of oppression in the context of particular social formations. This means that racism cannot be understood without reference to other social relations such as gender, class and sexuality. It also means that there is not one but numerous different racisms, that are continuously reworked and position black groups in different ways in particular social and historical contexts. For example, colonial racisms positioned black groups as biologically (and therefore culturally) inferior[1] and drew on particular ethnically differentiated ideological constructions of Africans as savage, and Arabs and Asians as heathen, backward and barbarous. These images relied powerfully on gender and sexuality as signifiers of particular 'racial' groups. Thus, where African women were conceptualised as animalistic in terms of their sexuality (see Donald and Rattansi, 1992), Arab women were portrayed as particularly guarding their sexuality, so as 'exotic' and 'full of Eastern promise'.

Contemporary racisms contain variants of old themes and draw on a range of discourses about inferiority and superiority, biology, culture and difference. Some of the images and ideas referred to above were reworked in the racialisation of immigration that took place from the

1950s onwards in England that presented immigration as a threat to a mythic 'British way of life' (see Barker, 1981). Thus at various points since 1950, discourses on race have positioned different sections of the black community as criminals, drug dealers and pimps (African-Caribbean men), prostitutes, single mothers (African-Caribbean women) fundamentalists, cheats and hotheads, welfare scroungers (Asian men), welfare dependants who breed like rabbits and threaten to use up resources (Asian women). And current discourses position Muslims as terrorists and asylum seekers as bogus.

Running through these various racisms is a discourse of *cultural pathology*. This implies that something is inherently inferior in the familial and cultural background of those from minority ethnic or black groups. This discourse problematises such groups and positions them in a relationship of inferiority to a white majority group. Yet it also relies on the construction of difference between groups within the black category. So for example, the culture and family life of African-Caribbean families is currently depicted as problematic because of an apparent lack of discipline and absence of family ties. For Asian families it is a concern with 'too much' discipline that supports this pathological reading and here the family is constructed as particularly tightly knit. According to the discourse, particular problems arise for Asian youth from the constraints imposed by familial and cultural requirements. Asian girls are positioned as shy, timid and passive and as somehow caught between the conflicting cultures of the school (which is equated with freedom) and the home (which represents restriction to the traditional role).

While this discourse has been subjected to criticism in academic writing over the last two decades it remains a powerful and central reference point in the wider and popular constructions of Asian family life and of Asian femininity in particular. A brief examination of some of the dominant media representations of Asian femininity will illustrate my point.

RACIALISED DISCOURSES
East *vs.* West: a recipe for culture clash

Back in 1984, Pratibha Parmar referred to the contradictory media images of Asian women, as on the one hand as 'sexually erotic creatures' who are 'full of Eastern Promise', and on the other as dominated by their men. This, according to Parmar, resulted in overall representations of them as meek, passive and tradition bound.

Although this image of the meek and tradition bound Asian woman continued into the 1990s, this decade also saw the birth of the *Asian babe*, as an extension of the exotic image of Asian women. Initially this term was associated with pornographic images of Asian women exemplified in the early 1990s in features on Muslim strippers (see Khanum, 1995), pornographic films featuring young Asian women (see Bhattia, 1991), and photographic images (*Asian Babes* magazine)[2]. The Asian babe label however, went onto take a wider and more subtle meaning by referring to the image of the exotic, dusky maiden. High profile women such as Pamela Bordes and Sunita Russel – one time escort of restauranter Sir Terence Conran – were considered leading Asian babes (see Knight, 1993; Russel, 1993).

While it is now more commonplace to see Asian women in a variety of roles in the media (particularly in broadcasting) *young* Asian women and especially those under 18 remain largely invisible or, when present, are there by reference to particular themes. These include forced or arranged marriages, domineering fathers, cultural practices such as purdah[3] and more generally culture clash.

In much of this reporting, the main 'problems' faced by Asian girls are seen as resulting from their strict upbringing, where fathers listen in to their conversations and girls are forced to marry strangers and sporadically take days off from school. Asian girls in the classroom apparently have limited ideas because of their cultures (see for example Wilce, 1984; Brah, 1996). While there are numerous examples of such representations of Asian femininity and of Asian youth generally, I wish to focus here mainly on two media texts (though I refer briefly to others) separated by some ten years to support my argument.

The first is an article which appeared in the *Times Educational Supplement* (*TES*) in 1991 that I came across while I was working as Graduate Teaching Assistant on an Educational and Professional Studies course with Teacher Trainees (now associates). I was particularly struck by the response the article invoked, with the majority of students (now qualified teachers) finding it extremely difficult to accept the critical reading of it that I present below. Instead they appeared to find it easier to feel extremely sorry for the Asian girl and others who are similarly downtrodden. The second is the film *East is East* which was hailed as a success for race relations but which reproduces familiar themes associated with the cultural pathology discourse of domestic violence, domineering fathers, passive Asian women and the East/West culture clash.

Culture clash on their plate

The main focus of the *Times Educational Supplement* article (Pugh, 1991) is the apparently 'surprising rate of anorexia nervosa and bulimia among British Asian girls'. It features a picture of a young girl in Muslim head-dress captioned 'a Bradford Asian girl'. The article itself begins with a description of the experiences of fourteen-year-old Amina from Bradford who is described as 'normal in school' because she is 'preoccupied with boys and last night's television'. We are told that when she leaves the school gates, however, she walks into another world entirely:

> Her teacher father does not allow her out after school, ruling out aerobic classes, birthday parties and visits to the cinema with friends. She spends the next three hours helping her mother prepare intricate curry dishes before doing her homework. She resents this because the same rules do not apply to her thirteen-year-old brother. He is out several times a week and has even been to a disco...When she visited her parents' family in India a year ago she came inescapably face to face with Asian culture. She wore Asian clothing and became submissive as was expected. (Pugh, 1991: 10)

Throughout the article Asian culture is defined explicitly and implicitly as constraining. It is argued that within it, Asian girls feel they lack control, which in turn causes anorexia. This argument itself is underpinned by the idea that western youth culture is 'freer' than Asian cultures. It is suggested that Amina's brother has tasted more of this freedom because he has visited a disco.

The idea that western youth culture is freer is open to question. As Parmar and Amos (1981) have noted, the usefulness of concepts such as *freedom, choice* and *arrangement* is open to debate. For western women who are pressured to go to discos to find a partner, it could equally be argued that they have little freedom. Transcending the barriers of class in terms of marriage relations is highly improbable for most working class women, though it may be a possibility for a minority. It is also questionable whether waxing legs and bikini lines or squeezing into tight dresses could be construed as free.

The idea that all 14 year old girls should be preoccupied with boys is also highly simplistic. Many heterosexual girls are certainly not pre-occupied with boys at this or any age, and the article denies the experiences of young women who experience uncertainty about their sexuality and of lesbian women.[4]

Amina's mother is notably absent in the article, excepting in reference to curry dishes, which effectively marginalises Asian women to a domestic role. Amina is therefore portrayed as at the mercy of her father who, despite being a teacher, is represented as the undisputed head of household. We are told that he imposes restrictions on her freedom and denies her the privileges afforded by western society, which she experiences only at school. Having drawn the frame of reference within a pathology model, the author proceeds to discuss the possible reasons for such an alarming rate of eating disorders among young Asian women.

> The theory is that with excessive slimming the individual can exert power over her body, expressing revolt against a parental regime, which frowns upon the freer western youth culture. (*ibid*)

There is no mention in the article of the role played by racism in the young women's daily lives. Instead, the blame for the disease is laid firmly at the door of Asian cultures. It is only in the final paragraph of the article that an alternative view is expressed. An 'expert' psychologist, Rachel Bryant Waugh is quoted as saying:

> It is much more important to view anorexia and bulimia as a means of coping with some stressful situation. In these girls it is a cultural conflict but if you take it away they could get it because of something else. (*ibid*)

Not even at this stage is it acknowledged that racism or sexism in the wider western cultures might be contributory factors to a such a 'stressful situation'. It is recognised towards the end of the article that the disease is not directly caused by a refusal to integrate into western society but by this stage this is marginalised and carries relatively little weight in the context of an article which is based on the supposition that all Asian girls are the victims of the cultures in which they are raised, cultures within which they are dominated by men.

East is East

Culture clash is also a central theme in the film *East is East*, shown in cinemas across the UK in 2000. Based on Asif Din Khan's stage play of the same name, this film tells the story of a Pakistani chip shop owner 'George' Khan, who lives with his English wife Ella and seven children whom he wishes to bring up in a traditional Pakistani 'way of life'.

Set in 1970s Salford, the story opens with a traditional Muslim wedding scene from which the eldest son, Nazir, flees. We learn that he was being forced (by his father) into this marriage. The remaining six children, including Meenah the only daughter, reject every aspect of Pakistani Muslim culture and family life. They rebel by eating pork and bacon when their father is out of the house and, in the case of Tariq – the second eldest son – by sneaking out to the local disco after hours. As in the culture clash article, the disco, as the symbol of western youth culture, represents the freedom that is denied the children by their overbearing father.

George is portrayed as a domineering father who controls his family with threat of violence and is frequently abusive, for example, calling them 'Bastard'. The film also features a particularly graphic scene of physical violence where George sets upon Ella as she attempts to defend her sons. The scene takes place after the children discover that their father has secretly planned a double wedding for two of his sons, Tariq and Afsal. The brides to be are the daughters of Bradford butcher Mr. Khan, who is recommended to George by a friend in mosque. As with other decisions, the suggestion is that George bases his decisions on the desire to be accepted within his culture, which effectively means that the individuality of his children is disregarded.

George's daughter Meenah is depicted as a tomboy who is most comfortable in her western clothing but is forced by her father to wear traditional dress – which she despises – at weekends. In stark contrast to Meenah, other young Asian women are notably silenced and/or presented in a negative way. For example, the girls whom the brothers are to wed by arrangement are literally denied a voice throughout the film. They never speak, are portrayed as extremely ugly, and symbolise all that is being rejected by George's westernised children; they are subjected to ridicule particularly for their appearance. A combination of these features is applied in one way or another to all traditionally dressed Asian women in the film. In fact, the only traditionally dressed Asian woman who is allowed a voice is Mrs Khan, the mother of the prospective brides. She is depicted as extremely condescending and is ridiculed when a sexually explicit piece of art belonging to one of George's sons (Saleem) lands on her lap.

In presenting this reading of *East is East,* I do not deny its attempt to deal critically with the theme of racism – it features for example a scene in which Meenah kicks a football into neighbour's window bearing a poster of Enoch Powell. However, the central characters (George's children) are firmly positioned outside of Pakistani culture. They actively reject their Pakistani identity by dissociating themselves from the culture and by habitually employing the racist term of abuse 'Paki' to describe other Pakistanis. But rather than being a 'success for race-relations' (Spencer, 2000), I would suggest that *East is East,* by repeating the familiar themes of arranged marriages, domestic violence, tradition versus 'progress', does just the opposite.

These analyses are of texts which portray Muslims and Pakistanis but the discourse of culture pathology extends to other groups in the Asian category. In an article featured in *The Independent* 'Miss Asia Looses Culture Clash' (14 February 1993) it is the Sikh community that is portrayed as backward and barbarous, because of its attempts to foil a beauty contest that was supposed to have been held in Birmingham in 1993.

Beauty contests, commonly regarded as degrading for women in general, are here portrayed as a potentially liberating experience which has been denied the girls by religious fundamentalists. As with Meenah in *East is East,* it is clear from the extract below that the wearing of western clothing symbolises defiance and resistance to strict parental regimes and culture. Traditionally dressed Asian girls lose their individuality and pale into insignificance:

> ... a couple of hundred Asian young women in traditional dress *huddled together,* anxious to avoid the press cameras because most of them had lied to their parents about where they were ... Sally Gill and Kim Uppall, both married and with professional jobs ... turned up anyway, partly in the hope that the modelling agencies might appear, and partly to vent their anger. They were *defiantly* wearing their most Western outfits – tight black trousers and little jewelled boleros. (*ibid,* my emphasis)

Continuing this theme, but this time with reference to the Sikh and Hindu communities, an article in the March 1995 edition of *Cosmopolitan* set about tackling the question of 'Why Asian women still run away from home'. The sub-heading reads:

> Torn between two conflicting cultures, many British women with Asian roots reject their parents' traditional beliefs – only to find they loose their parents too. (Wise, 1995: 14)

Although many young people run away from home in reaction to family pressures, among other reasons, the article singles out the practices and traditions of Asians as particularly oppressive, making huge generalisations throughout about Sikh, Hindu and Muslim cultures. As with anorexia in the Culture Clash article, an attempt is made here to link the disproportionate number of suicides among Asian women in the 15-34 age range with 'oppressive' Asian cultures. In attempting this link the author refers to a particularly horrific case of what can happen to an Asian girl who does not conform to the wishes of her family. Such references were made in the 1970s and early 1980s when reports of Asian girls being killed for disobeying their fathers were frequent (Parmar, 1984).

> Twelve years ago ... a mother-in-law became enraged by what she saw as her daughter-in-law's persistently 'Western' ways. The young woman was a secretary who dressed in European fashion. The atmosphere in the house in Middlesex, where all the mother-in-law's sons lived with their wives, became very tense. A conference was held between the mother and her sons and the husband was instructed to murder his wife to stop her decline into Western ways. *Dutifully* the man went up to his bedroom and strangled his wife. Even the sons who disagreed with the action were *duty bound* to assist in the cover up as the family tried to convince the police that the girl had been the victim of a burglary gone wrong. (Wise, 1996:14, my emphasis)

I am not suggesting that such incidents never occur, for they do. However, there is a tendency for them to be over-reported in the media and with language and imagery, especially the notion of duty, which implies that individuals are forced to carry out such actions or practices in the name of their religion or culture. Asian girls are most commonly positioned as the victims of such practices or actions.

All this is to draw attention to the discursive construction of Asian femininity that I examine in later chapters as it plays out in the field of schooling. Because discourse at its simplest is language in action (Mulhern, 2000), an important consequence of adopting such a culturalist perspective is that it can become translated via common-sense into the routine practices of professionals (youth workers, teachers, careers officers and even academics (see chapter two), dealing with Asian girls as part of their work. The outcomes of these practices, whether intentional or unintentional, can produce effects that potentially limit the opportunities available to Asian girls.

Some teachers and careers officers armed with pathological assumptions – for example, that all young Asian women have arranged marriages – have been found to 'dampen' the careers aspirations of young women from Asian backgrounds (Parmar, 1988). The career aspirations of Asian girls may be defined as unrealistic by such teachers, because is assumed that cultural constraints prevent Asian girls from partaking in post compulsory schooling (Brah, 1985). These assumptions were fuelled in the 1980s by stories of Asian fathers refusing to sign grant forms (see *Times Educational Supplement* 16 April 1984) and continue to be fed by on-going debates about forced marriages (Samad and Eade, 2002). Teachers, careers officers and youth workers can, albeit unwittingly, become part of the process whereby the Asian girl is denied access to opportunities offered to other youth in the labour market.

Critiquing cultural pathology

A number of critiques can be applied to the discourse of cultural pathology. Firstly, when applied to Asian groups, the discourse of cultural pathology is fundamentally heterosexual. The assumption of arranged marriages presupposes heterosexuality as the norm in Asian families. Sonia Arora Madan of the pop band *Echobelly*, having found herself in the unusual position of being identified as a role model for young Asian women, commented on the issues that she was asked by the press to speak about:

> The attention is flattering, the questions are not. They all want to know about the same thing; they talk about marriage agencies – bureaux for arranged marriages – and ask about my ideal man, who I'd like to have as a husband. Obviously they presume I'm heterosexual, obviously I don't answer. (Arora Madan, cited in Raphael, 1994)

What Arora Madan highlights here is how the media, through its preoccupation with arranged marriages, neglects differences in sexual orientation among Asian women and girls. In addition to sexuality, there are other significant divisions between Asian groups that are neglected within the cultural pathology discourse.

A second problem with the cultural pathology framework is that it falsely homogenises Asian communities, thereby obscuring differences within and between Asian communities. The parents and grandparents of young Asian women have migrated from different parts of the Indian subcontinent and there are also different religious, linguistic patterns and castes associated with those areas, which may or may not inform the cultural practices of individual Asian families in Britain.

Asian groups have migrated from parts of Pakistan, India and Bangladesh. Pakistanis have migrated from three areas: the North Western Frontier Province, the Mirpuri border areas with Kashmir and the province of Punjab. Indians originate from the Punjab State and areas of the Gujerat and Kutch, whilst Bangladeshis have migrated from two main areas, the border with Assam (India) and the Maritime East India areas (Shah, 1992).

Pathans, Kashmiris (or Mirpuris) and Punjabis are the main ethnic groups originating from Pakistan. All three groups are predominantly Muslim and their languages are respectively Pushto, Mirpuri and Punjabi. Gujeratis and Punjabis are the main groups to have originated from India. Indian Punjabis are predominately Sikh, but a minority have adopted the Hindu faith. The majority of Gujeratis are Hindu but Gujerati Muslims also originate from India. Sikhs are also Punjabi speakers and Hindus Gujerati speakers. Many Punjabi Sikhs and Muslims have lived in East Africa before coming to Britain, as have some Indian Hindus and Muslims. Sylhetis and Bengalis originate from Bangladesh and are overwhelmingly Muslim. However, there are also Bangladeshi Hindus living in Britain (Shah, 1992; Taylor, 1985). Commission for Racial Equality (CRE, 2001) statistics show that there are almost two million Muslims resident in Britain, compared with 400,000 Hindus and 400,000 Sikhs.

In addition to the differences of language, religion and region of origin, gender patterns vary within Asian households and may cut across the differences outlined above. Class differences also exist, resulting from their families' positions prior to migration, from the occupations pursued within Britain and also regional variations in the cultures which Asian young women inhabit (Brah, 1993; Bhachu, 1991). The majority of Pakistanis are concentrated in the West Midlands (21%) and in Yorkshire and Humberside (20%). The majority of the Bangladeshi population lives in Greater London (54%) and the West Midlands (12%). Indians, while more widely spread, have large concentrations in the South East (53%) and the Midlands (30%) (CRE, 1999a).

A third problem with the cultural pathology discourse is that the exclusive focus on culture, and particularly on so-called oppressive patriarchal relations within Asian communities, obscures the role that is played by racism and racial harassment in the lives of Asian girls. Consequently, attention is diverted from wider questions of social justice and equality. It is this point that I wish to focus on next, with reference briefly to the two policy settings of criminal justice and education.

Racism, criminal justice and educational policy
In the week that saw the beating half to death of Quaddus Ali in the east end of London, Sunita Russel wrote an article on the subject of being an Asian Babe in the *The Times* of 10 September 1993, entitled 'The Empire Strikes Back'. In it she described the advantages Asian women enjoy because they are 'dusky' and have a 'natural tan'. She went on to make the claim that: 'We Asian Aphrodites are welcomed into British society without even a hint of racism'.

While it may be true that some Asian girls and women are in a fortunate position of never experiencing racism or being aware of it, this is certainly not the case for all Asian girls and women, for many of whom racial attack is a real threat. As Knight argued in reply:

> No darling! We Asian Aphrodites join the Anti Nazi league because we know there are people out there whose idea of fun is sticking a size 11 DM into our pretty, doe eyed faces. (Knight, 1993:8)

According to the CRE, who define racial harassment as verbal or physical aggression towards individuals and attacks on property or groups because of race, nationality, ethnic or national origin, Asians are the largest group of victims of racial harassment. In 1992, there were 130,000 racially motivated crimes, 41,000 against black groups and 89,000 against Asians (CRE, 1995). In 1997/8 the police recorded 130,878 racial incidents against victims from all ethnic groups in England and Wales. This was an increase of 6% on the previous year but fell far short of the 382,0000 crimes estimated by the 1996 British Crime Survey as having been motivated by racism (CRE, 1999b).

Racial harassment is, however, only one aspect of the racism so utterly marginalised by the cultural pathology discourse, and which impacts differentially on Asian girls' schooling and identity. In a review of a number of surveys in the fields of education, housing, social security, employment and the criminal justice system in 1991, the Campaign Against Racism and Fascism (CARF) concluded that:

> Black people are systematically denied equal and fair treatment and are discriminated against in all areas of life. (CARF, 1991:8)

Almost a decade later the report of the Stephen Lawrence murder inquiry (Macpherson, 1999) endorsed this finding and called for public sector organisations (principally the police, but others too, including the education service) to examine their practices and to implement policies to tackle institutional racism[5].

For a short period after the report's publication it seemed that there was genuine willingness in the public sphere to embrace Macpherson's definition of institutional racism, the report's contents and more importantly the need to put words into action. This euphoria was short-lived however, as within weeks of its publication the report was subjected to widespread media and public criticism (see Blair *et al,* 1998 for a discussion).

A number of years on, it seems that Macpherson's recommendations have not yet been translated into practice. In the criminal justice sector for example, New Labour may have introduced 'performance indicators of specialist training and targets on ethnic recruitment to the force' but...

> Nothing has been done to dismantle one of the most resented and blatantly police practices, stop and search, in which black men are six times more likely than their white peers to be picked up. (Sivanandan, 2000:69)

CRE statistics suggest that African-Caribbean men are the most likely to stopped and searched, at least five times more likely than white men). Although the figures for Asian men are variable, they are as proportionally high in some regions. This, alongside high unemployment rates and widespread poverty in some parts of England were contributory factors to the inner-city disturbances in the northern towns and cities of Oldham, Burnley Bradford and Stoke in the summer of 2001 (CARF, 2001). An interim report on employment published by the Cabinet

Office in February 2002 revealed that Muslim men of Pakistani and Bangladeshi origin, who are predominantly located in the 'racial hot-spots' are disproportionately unemployed relative to other groups in-cluding other Asians of non Muslim backgrounds (see Walker, 2002). Even after allowing for education and residential area, Pakistani Muslims are three times more likely to be unemployed than Hindus, Indian Muslims twice more likely than Indian Hindus. This is a measure of the deprivation in these areas.

In education, New Labour responded to Macpherson by releasing Ofsted's (1999) *Raising the attainment of minority ethnic pupils – School and LEA responses* just weeks after the publication of the Stephen Lawrence Inquiry Report. This consists of a report focusing on raising achievement with reference to school and LEA responses and secondly, guidance on the same issue for providers of Initial Teacher Training (ITT). It is based on primarily on Ofsted research (Gillborn and Gipps, 1996) and *Taking Steps*, the third report of the Racial Attacks Group (Home Office, 2000) and reveals two important find-ings. The first is that not all black children underachieve. Instead it identifies four main groups within the category of minority ethnic who are deemed to be underachieving (Bangladeshi, Black Caribbean, Pakistani, Gypsy traveller). The second is that many of the schools pro-viding for these students serve communities that are characterised

> ...by socio-economic disadvantage, with high unemployment, over-crowded housing, environmental deprivation (including limited safe play areas for children), high levels of racial tension and rapidly changing popu-lations. Eligibility for free school meals was nearly always high, usually twice the national average but sometimes much higher. (Ofsted, 1999:5)

This would suggest that socio-economic factors rather than ethnicity alone are important to understanding the 'under-performance' of such groups. Despite this apparent recognition however, the remainder of the document focuses attention mainly on school-based initiatives and pri-marily on the collection and monitoring of statistical data on under-achievement as a way of tackling the issue. This approach is reflective of New Labour's wider policy framework for education which links education to issues of global competitiveness. This requires an em-phasis on the promotion of achievement as the solution to social ex-clusion and disadvantage (Ozga, 1999) and sees school effectiveness and improvement as the model approach for schools towards the promotion of achievement. Within this framework, policies which many researchers (Gewirtz, 1998) have shown to discriminate against black and working class children (such as setting by ability) continue to be promoted as the way forward for schools (Kenny, 1999). As Blair et al have argued,

> ...the current forces driving national education policy have little regard for the problems of institutional racism. Indeed the fetishization of league tables and 'standards' measured by the crudest terms possible actually produces exactly the circumstances whereby institutional racism flourishes. (Blair *et al*, 1998: 9)

New Labour's policy for education as also exemplified in key documents such as *Excellence in Cities* (DfEE, 1997) and the Green paper *Schools Building on Success* (DfEE, 2001) therefore places the emphasis firmly on 'standards not structures'. That is, on measurable indicators of success rather than widespread concerns with issues of inequality and social injustice. Like much of the school improvement literature, to which it is intimately connected in the search for successful performance, this policy shifts attention from wider economic and political questions. As Angus has argued, it fails 'to explore the relationship of specific practices to wider social and cultural constructions and political and economic interests' (1993:335). In doing so it downplays the significance of class, race and gender, all of which, as I argue in this book are significant factors in the schooling and identity Asian girls.

GENDERED DISCOURSES

Current discourses on Asian masculinity are central to the positioning of Asian girls as the passive victims of oppressive cultures and the inner city disturbances of 2001 and the 'war on terrorism' have further reinforced a set of images of young Asian men as fundamentalist, hotheaded, volatile and aggressive. The increasing focus on Islam as a perceived threat to global capitalism since the demise of communism and the eastern block has served to strengthen arguments about the threat to British culture posed by barbaric religious and cultural practices associated with black immigration after the second world war. Since the 1960s the state has played a central and active role in shaping political debates about immigrants and their cultures. I briefly discuss this racialisation of immigration (see Solomos, 1992; Layton-Henry, 1992) for a fuller discussion) before focusing on racialised discourses on black youth since the 1980s. Against the background of changing economic and political forces, Asian youth have increasingly come under the spotlight. I explore some key events that have been central in the racialisation of religion and show that it has had a significant impact on schooling because of its re-positioning of Muslims groups and Asian boys and men as the 'enemy within'.

The racialisation of immigration

Black commonwealth immigrants arriving in Britain to help Britain re-build the economy after the second world war initially received a warm welcome but were soon to be treated with suspicion and hostility, particularly in the workplace as competition for jobs grew. Throughout the period 1948 to the 1960s public and private debates began to focus on the problems of black immigration. Discussion centred on high numbers and on the impact of black immigration on housing, the welfare state, crime and social problems. Black groups came to be viewed as undesirable and were openly cited as bringing with them certain social problems, prostitution and drug-related crime, particularly so in the case of African-Caribbeans (Anwar, 1986; Solomos, 1992; Layton-Henry, 1992). The immigration issue became racialised: the debate was not only about the characteristics of black people but the effect of black immigration on the racial character of white people and on 'the national identity' – the 'British way of life'. These themes were clearly to be seen in the aftermath of the Notting Hill and Nottingham riots in August and September 1958. Although it was the black community that was attacked by whites, the debates in the media focused particularly on the dangers of unrestricted immigration, pushing the blame onto the black communities themselves. The racialisation of immigration was achieved in a coded way such that race was not always mentioned but 'immigrant' became synonymous with 'problem'. The misuse of language became so prevalent that even black people born in Britain were assumed to be immigrants.

Solomos (1992) has argued that the state played a 'central role in defining both the form and the content of policies and wider political agendas'. Indeed the state and its agencies have become the locus of struggle over the forms of political regulation of immigration and the management of domestic relations' (1992:26). Political controls since the 1960s have relied heavily on a particular racist ideology which, unlike the racism of the colonial period, does not view blacks as inferior but as culturally different. This 'new racism' (Barker, 1981) draws on sociobiological concepts such as kin altruism (herd instinct) legitimising the need to protect ones' own kind from alien invasion, thus naturalising racism. According to this viewpoint, the 'genuine fears' of ordinary people that their country may be swamped by people with alien cultures and lifestyles are justified; this theory reverses the charges so that a racist becomes someone who does not adopt the lifestyle and culture of the host nation.

Gender has been central to the new racism. Fear of swamping invokes the imagery of black women breeding like rabbits. The Asian woman in racist imagery is characterised as the passive, subservient, dependent wife walking three paces behind her husband and, more potently, as the bearer of backward alien cultures which threaten to undermine the social order. These images are also rooted in Britain's imperial past, when Asian women in the days of colonialism were seen as passive and quiet and in need of liberation. Such arguments provided a justification of the civilising mission in which white women played a central role (Ware, 1992).

While the immigration issue focused heavily on race, in the discourse on youth race concerns were secondary to the problem of youth. But from the mid 1970s, as the Thatcher government prepared to take office, a new racialised discourse was constructed which positioned black youth as the enemy within. By the mid 1980s black youth were being characterised as a 'social time bomb' (see Solomos and Back, 1996). The transformation of inner city areas in relation to economic and social structures provided possibilities for the racialisation of such issues as employment, housing, education and the law. This racialisation process moved the focus of debate from immigration itself to the identification of social 'problems' linked to race, particularly in relation to young blacks in education, the police and urban policy (Centre for Contemporary Cultural Studies, 1982).

The idea that black youth were a 'social time bomb' (Solomos and Back, 1996) was strengthened by the inner city disturbances in Brixton, Handsworth and Liverpool in 1981 and 1985. These inner city disturbances were interpreted by the press and by the former Conservative

MP Enoch Powell, as intimately linked to the size and concentration of the black population in certain areas. African Caribbean youth were the main focus of such arguments; even though a second generation of Asians was already reacting against the passivity they attributed the first generation of settlers. The resistance of Asian youth to the experience of being victimised is now well documented (Sivanandan, 1981; Parmar, 1982). Resistance to attack has also taken many forms, from the individual actions of Asian children against 'Paki-bashing' to more organised mass resistance. The Race Today Collective (1983) reported on various youth campaigns in the 1970s in, for example the mass squatting over housing between 1972-75 in Southall and Bradford. The Southall Youth Movement was formed in 1978 after the racist murder of Gurdip Singh Chaggar (Bains, 1988) and in 1981, Bradford youth were brought to trial for organised resistance against fascists.

Despite these numerous examples of resistance, Asian youth were generally characterised as passive yet hardworking, happy yet seriously studious, compared with the image of Brixton's African Caribbean young men 'who had been playing a new and gruesome variation of cricket using bricks for balls and plastic police shields for bats' (Gilroy and Lawrence, 1988:121-2, see also Back, 1994:11-13).

The late 1980s, however, marked the beginning of a new era in the positioning of Asian youth as extremely volatile, violent, angry and hotheaded. While this shift cannot be explained by one event or cause alone, it is clear that what came to be known as the Rushdie affair in England had a significant impact on the racialisation of religion which is central to the ways young Asians are viewed today. It is worth examining the controversy and subsequent events, to put this racialisation process into context.

The *Satanic Verses* controversy

The Rushdie affair has played a crucial role in the politicisation of Muslim identity. Groups previously identified and identifying themselves as variously Pakistani, Mirpuri, Punjabi, Indian, have since been defined primarily by religion, that is, as Muslims (Saghal and Yuval-Davis, 1992).

The *Satanic Verses* controversy began in 1988 with the publication of a novel in which Salman Rushdie explores the themes of cultural alienation, racism and the role of religion. The strong opposition to the book was based upon the thin line it drew between fact and fiction. Rushdie cast doubts on the authenticity of the *Quoran*, implying that parts of it were the work of the devil. It was in England, and particularly in Bradford, that the strongest reaction to the book was manifest. Although the first book-burning was held in Bolton in December 1988, when 7,000 people staged a demonstration, the greatest publicity and condemnation was directed at the famous book-burning in Bradford in January 1989. On February 14th 1989, the Ayatollah issued his *fatwa*, leading to a dramatic turn in events as demonstrations against the book led to scenes of anger, violence and destruction in many parts of the world. But it was the participation of *young Asian men* in places such as Bradford that grabbed the attention of observers and social analysts.

The fact that young Asian men were at the forefront of the demonstrations and scenes of anger in places such as Bradford cannot be explained in terms of religion alone. As Samad (1992) and Malik (1989) have argued, if this had been the case then all parts of England which have sizable Muslim populations would have responded in a similar way. But the involvement of the Bangladeshis in East London was restricted to two marches in Hyde Park, there was no apparent increase in religiosity – the restaurants still served alcohol and attendance for prayer in the mosques remained thin (Samad, 1992). Indeed, Malik (1989) argues that many of the young protesters were not religious at all. Few could recite the *Quoran* and many, he argues, were as British as their white peers, for instance, not observing the taboos around drinking and sex.

The controversy needs then to be understood in relation to other factors, central to which is the location in Bradford of particular communities divided by class, race, religion, language and *biraderis*, where Mirpuris are in the majority. Samad (1992) argues that the affair was primarily racial. The Mirpuri working class, particularly the young, had been radicalised by a decade of racial provocations. The 1970s recession led to competition for jobs and the Asian community was singled out for its obvious racial, religious and cultural differences. Various organisations, such as the Azad Kashmir Muslim Association and the Asian Youth Movement, had persistently argued during the late 1970s that racial tension in Bradford was increasing, as was the activity of the British

National Party, the National Front and the Yorkshire Campaign to Stop Immigration, and racial attacks, fights and arson attacks.

The whole issue came to a head in 1981 with the case of the Bradford Twelve, when youth of Indian and Pakistani origin were arrested for being in possession of incendiary devices. Defendants claimed that the petrol bombs were for self-defence against the threatened skinhead attack on their community. Samad observes that their 'trial drew a graphic picture of a community under constant fear of attack, with hardly any offer of police protection' (Samad, 1992:512). The defendants were proved innocent. However, the deterioration in race relations continued when Ray Honeyford, Headteacher of Drummond Middle School made inflammatory assertions, particularly about the Mirpuri community, accusing them of bringing down standards in his school.

These two incidents, according to Samad, became powerful push factors among the young Mirpuris who were searching for a vehicle to voice their discontent. He argues that the young Pakistanis' hurt and anger lingering after the Honeyford affair was exacerbated by the *Satanic Verses* issue, which was perceived as another gratuitous insult. 'It was the perception that they were again humiliated which was responsible for making religious consciousness dominant over identities' (*ibid*:516).

The banning of *International Guerrillas*, a video film in which a Rushdie-like figure was crucified, was thus read by Bradford youth as hypocritical. Samad argues:

> The frustrations and indignation which was present in the Mirpuri community and the unwillingness of society to give them a fair deal left them deeply dissatisfied. Thus, when the international campaign against Rushdie was radicalised by Tehran, it allowed the religious leadership to steal a march over their secular rivals and draw in <u>angry young men</u> into the agitation. Combined with other issues such as blasphemy laws and the demand for Muslim schools it allowed the divines to set the agenda for the community. (Samad, 1992:516, my emphasis)

So it was not just religion but material and social conditions underpinning the decade of racial provocation that made this a peculiarly Bradford affair. Nor was it just angry young men who took stance on this issue; young women could be found both in support of Rushdie and against him but they received significantly less attention than the boys and men.

The role of women in the controversy

Although some women agreed with the anti-Rushdie stance and saw the novel as an attack on the Muslim religion, a view expressed openly by Rana Kabbani (1989), others were opposed to what they viewed as religious fundamentalism interfering in their lives. The Women Against Fundamentalism (WAF) group, for example, was founded in May 1989, with its founding statement calling for 'the separation of state and religion in Britain as a precondition for defeating fundamentalism' (WAF, 1989). Hanna Siddiqui, a member of WAF, takes issue with Rana Kabbani's book in which she writes about the damaging effect of Rushdie's book to the antiracist struggle. Siddiqui argues that Kabbani's book:

> ... denies the experiences of many ordinary Asians living in Britain, espe-
> cially women, who have been castigated and censored for expressing
> doubt and dissent within their families and communities. It neglects the
> feminist struggles of Asian women across the world who have been fight-
> ing against the imposition of religious values in their lives. (Siddiqui, 1991:
> 80)

In May 1989, the women-only group decided to picket the anti-Rushdie march in London and found themselves caught between the National Front (NF) on the one hand and the anti-Rushdie group on the other.

> The head of the march had been successfully contested by a group of
> young men carrying pro-Khomeini banners and wearing the insignia of
> religious warriors. They were already excited by their tussles with the
> elders and police. When they heard our piercing whistles and saw our
> banners 'Religious leaders don't speak for us', 'Rushdie's right to write is
> ours to dissent' they turned on us in fury ... But we regrouped further
> back in the square, and spent a further hour entertaining the media by
> fending off the attempts of the National Front milling around fruitlessly ...
> ignored by the marchers, they turned on us ... (Connolly, 1991:71)

What this clearly illustrates is that there were more than two sides in the *Satanic Verses* controversy. But it is the outcome that is of significance for Asians in England.

The Rushdie affair served as a focus for public and political debates about preserving 'our' (white British) way life, our values of freedom and liberalism against the alien, uncivilised, uncultured, mysogynistic beings (Muslims) we live among in a multicultural society. As the pressure on immigrants to conform and assimilate was articulated 'above', it was interpreted in a different way 'below' in the form of attacks on Muslims. In the Darnell area of Sheffield, Muslim homes and a mosque were attacked in the wake of the Rushdie affair. In London, the Regents Park mosque was firebombed and in 1993 the Saddam Hussein mosque in Birmingham was damaged (see issues of CARF Journal, 1993). At the level of discourse, the Rushdie affair enabled old ideas of the backwardness of Muslims, to be revived and reactivated though racist common-sense.

Asian girls and young women were characterised as the most visible symbols and victims of this backwardness because of the re-emergence of the violent image of Asian men. Particularly significant for schooling was that the controversy also added a new racist term of abuse, *Rushdie,* which conjured up images of mad Muslims refusing to integrate into a society which has tolerated them thus far. There was also a shift in the meaning of *Paki* to mean Muslim rather than Asian, although this is not always clearly distinguished in the minds of those doing the name-calling. People attacked at this time were not only Muslims but anyone who appeared to be like them.

Like the Rushdie affair, the Gulf War of 1991 has also had a lasting legacy where representations of Muslim communities are concerned. In schools, too, children experienced heightened tensions because public reaction to the war resonated with the negative racialised imagery begun by the Rushdie affair.

The Gulf War 1991

Operation Desert Storm, the international mission to 'liberate' Kuwait, began on January 16th. Iraq was bombed by an alliance which included the UK as part of Western Europe, and the US. As with the Rushdie affair, communities polarised. Many young Asians, male and female, supported Iraqi president, Saddam Hussein, neither because they believed in his cause nor because they practiced the Muslim religion but because doing so signified an act of defiance to a British social structure which had systematically excluded them from its benefits. There are parallels here between this and the support for Osama Bin Laden in many parts of the globe.

As with the Rushdie affair, the effect of the Gulf crisis on the social imagery of Asians was profound. In the media, images of barbarism, and irrationality were brought to the fore. Saddam Hussein was referred to as the 'butcher of Baghdad', a 'madman', and 'evil villain', like Gadaffi of Libya before him. More than ever, people of Arab-like appearance or of Muslim backgrounds were asked to indicate where their sympathies lay. It all echoed the 'Cricket Test' proposed by Norman Tebbit, Conservative MP, whereby supporting a team pitted against the English team was read as a refusal to integrate into British society. We have seen that in the post September 11 context, David Blunkett was also able to re-work such arguments with reference to the linguistic and cultural practices of sections of the Asian community in the UK.

During the time of the Gulf war, the CRE reported a sharp rise in incidents of anti-Muslim violence (Layton-Henry, 1992). There was an increase in anti-Islamic feeling which was inflamed by an astonishingly jingoistic stance in tabloids. The editor of the *Daily Star* wrote 'It is time to deport fanatical Muslims baying for the death of our boys in the Gulf'. The tabloid's reaction to Winston Churchill's (MP for Davyhulme) speeches on immigration in May and July 1993 was also interesting. Churchill described 'the relentless flow of Muslims' he was fighting on 'our beaches'. Spark in the *Mail on Sunday* spoke of Churchill's courage in breaking the 'race taboo' that had ensured a 'conspiracy of silence on racial problems'. Brian Hitchin in the *Daily Star* criticised 'the hypocrisy machine' that 'shoved Winston Churchill through the mincer' for having 'the courage to say the unsayable'. Kilroy-Silk in the *Daily Express* wrote: 'Churchill deserves a tolerant hearing' and averred that Churchill had asked 'perfectly reasonable questions' and that criticisms of him demonstrated our 'lack of confidence in the maturity and tolerance of our democracy' (cited in CARF July/August 1993).

Kilroy-Silk also commented on the fact that 'British soldiers fighting in the Gulf to liberate Kuwait were not allowed to hold Christian services for fear of offending Muslims. In the *Daily Mail*, Mihir Bose wrote that the Asian attitude which requests a version of their Muslim republic, has 'done measurably more damage' than Churchill's (CARF, 1993).

Although the focus was on the Gulf, these discourses resonated with broader arguments about the social problems at home brought by immigration. Not only were Muslim communities accused of misplaced loyalties but they were also charged with driving native Englanders back to very margins of their land. Churchill for example, said:

> The unhappiness, indeed bitterness of the indigenous population runs very deep in those areas of our inner cities where the native English find that they have become the ethnic minority in their own land and where their children have to attend schools which, not infrequently, are made up of 80 per cent or more ethnic minorities and where in consequence a traditional English, Christian education is not longer the norm. (*Guardian* 20 July 1993)

Despite the fact that very few schools contain such high populations of ethnic minority children, Churchill's pronouncements in the aftermath of Gulf war helped to keep the numbers game alive and feed into the genuine fears of the British public. By the time Churchill made this speech, a further emotive issue – the 1992 Cricket test between Pakistan and England in 1992 – had enabled a reconnection of the themes of race and nation and put the spotlight firmly on Asian boys and young men whose origins were in the subcontinent.

'Cheats' and 'hotheads': the 1992 cricket series between Pakistan and England

The 1992 Cricket series between England and Pakistan mirrored the racism in wider society and served to reinforce the contradictory representations of Asians in the media, as passive and hardworking or as hotheaded and volatile. But the discourse provoked by the row also drew particularly on the image of the sly Arab who is always looking to deceive (Fryer, 1985). There were numerous allegations of 'ball doctoring' and cheating which resulted in the Pakistanis being characterised as uncivilised, hostile and hotheaded, a stereotype usually attributed to African Caribbean youth. So much so that whatever the Pakistanis did on the field was interpreted through this lens. There was harsh condemnation of bowler Aquib Javed who was described by television commentators 'aggressive' and 'disgraceful' when he snatched his sweater from the umpire after a disagreement over the umpire's decision not to give 'out'. More significantly, the stereotype was generalised to Pakistani national character. The press particularly singled out Waqar Younis and Wasim Akram for cheating and being volatile. The criticism was about not just Pakistani cricket but Pakistani national character. Bob Willis, a former England bowler, argued:

> It's the way these Pakistanis are brought up to play their cricket. It's the nature of the beast. Everything is confrontational. They don't say sorry willingly and don't often accept they are in the wrong ... it's not part of their character. (cited in Searle, 1993:48)

Such judgements about the national character of Pakistan were taken up by Michael Henderson in the *Guardian*. Famous cricket commentator John Arlott was quoted by Henderson as saying that 'cricket reflects the personality and spirit of those who play it, and by extension, illuminates the national character'. Henderson then added his own comment: 'All summer long the Pakistanis have been wilful, capricious and hot headed' (*ibid*:48-49).

The press appeared to focus not on the match but on the national character of Pakistan. One writer even offered a socio-biological perspective, asserting that it was the quality of the national perspiration which gave the Pakistanis the advantage and that it was in fact, 'the certain properties in their sweat which achieve a superior polish, which in turn gained the extra swing' (*ibid*).

When Michael Atherton, the England Captain was later found to have cheated, the incident was dismissed as the action of 'a foolish young man'. But significantly he was branded as neither a cheat nor a hothead. And neither was his behaviour racialised.

The public condemnation of the Pakistani players as cheats and hotheads was not without consequence. Significantly, at the same time as the accusations of ball tampering, an Asian youth was shot and blinded in one eye by a racist gang in Harrow, North London. Three young Asian men were murdered during the summer of the series within six weeks of one another, the victims of racist violence in Britain: Ruhallah Aramesh in Thornton Green, Ashiq Hussein in Birmingham and Rohit Duggal in Greenwich (see CARF, 1992). Only one of these men was Muslim, signaling that the material consequences of ideological images can be, and are, far reaching. A direct link cannot be proved between social representations and the material consequences but in the context of heightened tension about race, it is quite likely that the attacks were sparked by the racialisation of religious groups in response to these events. Older notions of race had been re-worked and reactivated. These emerging discourses on Asian masculinity did not signal a replacement of one racism with another but the simultaneous operation of different racisms – that is cultural or religious racisms co-exist with those focusing on supposed biological characteristics (Goldberg, 1992).

My focus in this book is on the schooling and identity of Asian girls and one of the clearest indications of the ways in which wider discourses impact on schooling can be seen in a documentary film made for BBC's Panorama. *Underclass in Purdah* was aired on March 29th 1993, some months after the ball tampering episode. The documentary focused mainly on the current problems of educating Asian youth in the locality of Bradford and was based on the findings of a Policy Studies Institute (PSI) survey, *Britain's ethnic minorities*, which examined the apparent 'growing gap between Britain's ethnic minorities' in terms of educational achievement. One of the PSI's findings was that Indians performed better than Pakistanis and Bangladeshis in gaining school-leaving qualifications. The report suggested that young Asian men had 'problems' concerning drugs and crime and that they posed threats to authority figures, both in school and to the social fabric of Britain. In short the message was that young Muslims of Pakistani and Bangladeshi origin were not only the new underclass but a time bomb waiting to go off.

Of Asian girls the programme presented three main images: the 'battered wife', the 'prostitute' and the over-controlled teenager experiencing sexual freedom in the world outside the home. In each case references were made to particular Asian men who were responsible for the subjugation of the women. The stories presented were also interspersed with references to frequent visual images of young Asian men engaging in criminal activities such as drug-dealing and pimping.

The programme was heavily criticised by the Muslim press and the Mosques. Speaking on behalf of the Bradford Council of Mosques, Ishtiaq Ahmed stated that the programme painted a very negative picture, reinforcing popularly held misinformation and prejudices about the community. He argued that the National Front could not have done a better job in putting together this negative view of Muslims (cited in the *Runneymede Trust Bulletin* May, 1993). The Campaign Against Racism and Fascism (CARF) criticised both the report and the programme for diverting the blame for 'failure' away from structural racism and onto the cultures of Muslim communities. The PSI was less than content with the way Panorama had interpreted their findings. Tariq Modood, senior research fellow at the PSI, stated that the sensationalist approach adopted by the programme, far from alerting society to the condition of Muslims, had merely added to the vilification which they already suffer (CARF July/August 1993):

> The programme was framed by cinema verité footage of pimps, prostitutes, and pushers in ill-lit mean streets. No evidence at all was offered to show that this was typical or relevant ... In any case, the whole sensationalist approach of the programme will not produce the understanding and sympathy on which effective policies can be built.

The *Panorama* documentary mirrored and reinforced the representations of the backward Muslim already available in popular discourse. The images of domination, backwardness, barbarity and sexualities were not new. They date back to the period of European expansion in the 16th century when Asian (and Arab) religions and cultures were characterised as heathen and backward (Fryer, 1985; 1988; Lawrence, 1982). The conceptions are, however, reactivated and reworked to support racisms that construct Asian cultures and religions as a threat to the British way of life and, through George's Bush's speeches in the aftermath of September 11, 2001 – as a threat to civilisation itself.

The re-working of old imperialist images is of particular significance for Asian girls and their schooling. Asian girls when present in media discourse have been used to highlight the increasing barbarity of perceived oppressive male Asian culture. They have been portrayed as completely dominated by men and as caught between the backward cultures of the home and the freedom of western cultures. In the social representations of Asian women, racialised discourses articulate with those of gender and class. As Brah has argued:

> Whether she is exoticised, represented as ruthlessly oppressed, in need of liberation, or read as a victim/enigmatic emblem of religious fundamentalism, she is often perceived as the bearer of races and cultures that are constructed a inherently threatening to the presumed superiority of western civilisations. (Brah, 1993:447-8)

For Asian girls and women such images have become embedded in material practices. Asian women were reported to have been strongly encouraged to have abortions in order to curb the size of the black British population. There was also a high incidence of Asian women being given Depro Prevero, an injectable contraceptive (Klug, 1989; Parmar, 1982).

Schooling also plays an important role in mediating these broader discourses on Asian cultures. Asian girls who break school rules, for example, by leaving school premises at lunch times or getting into cars, are sometimes treated more harshly than their peers precisely because of historic assumptions surrounding their sexuality. It is assumed that they go wild because they are so restricted at home.

There are also serious consequences, as we shall see, for girls who do not conform to dominant stereotypes of Asian femininity – that is, of passivity. Those who 'chat back' are labelled as trouble-makers, and subjected to harsh treatment from both staff and their peers; in some cases their femininity is subject to masculinisation with its own, often violent consequences. The accounts presented in this book explore some of these consequences for Asian girls and their schooling. In the next chapter, however, I set out the theoretical framework that underpins the book.

Notes

1 See Banton (1997) for further discussion of this discourse which he terms *The Doctrine of Racial Typology*.

2 This was the subject of a television documentary for the BBC's East in January 1994).

3 This is the practice of observing modesty through for example from the social separation of the sexes through to the veiling of women.

4 For an account of young people's experiences of being gay or bisexual see Norris and Read (1985), see also Epstein and Johnson (1998).

5 This was defined as 'The collective failure of an organisation to provide an appropriate and professional service to people because of their colour, culture or ethnic origin. It can be seen or detected in processes attitudes and behaviour which amount to discrimination through unwitting prejudice, ignorance, thoughlessness and racist stereotyping which disadvantages minority ethnic people.

It persists because of the failure of the organisation openly and adequately to recognise and address its existence and causes by policy, example and leadership' (Macpherson, 1999:28).

2

Invisibility, pathology and identity

In the light of the current discourses on Asian femininity outlined so far, this chapter examines some of the ways in which Asian girls have been presented in academic literature. In much of the early British literature on youth, Asian girls were either invisible or presented in certain stereotypical ways with reference to the cultural pathology discourse already discussed. From the 1980s onwards, the writing was concerned with challenging this negative stereotyping by focusing on 'resistance' strategies employed by Asian girls to deal with their experiences of schooling but it tended to ignore internal struggles and divisions within the *Asian* category. Since the 1990s and against the background of debates on identity, research studies on Asian girls and young women generally focus specifically on one sub group only, (eg Muslims, Sikhs). My argument is that in order to understand Asian girls' experiences of schooling it is important to take into account both the divisions and commonalities that exist, and to also recognise that the experiences of Asian girls are shaped by a multiplicity of factors such as race, ethnicity, class, gender, religion and region.

Invisibility and pathology – early British work on youth

With its predominant focus on the experiences of young working class males (Spinley, 1953; Sprott *et al*, 1954; Mays, 1954; Kerr, 1958; Downes, 1966, Cotsgrove and Parker, 1963; Willis, 1977; Corrigan, 1976) the early British sociological literature on youth did not feature Asian girls. Feminist analyses (McRobbie and Garber, 1976; Smart, 1976; Cambell, 1981; Leonard, 1987, Heidensohn, 1985; Griffin, 1986; Cain, 1989; McRobbie, 1991) pointed to the invisibility or absence of young women and to their marginal treatment when they were mentioned. This was because youth cultural studies took young men's experiences as the universal norm. This resulted in the advancement of gender specific theories (which were also white and heterosexual) and therefore could not be applied to young women (Griffin, 1986; McRobbie, 1991). Feminist research, however, focused primarily on young white women and thereby excluded accounts of black women, while studies of black youth focused on African-Caribbean young males (Hall *et al*, 1978; Dodd, 1978; Gutzmore, 1983; Gilroy, 1982; 1987). By reducing the experiences of young people in relation to only either gender, race or class, early youth studies effectively marginalised young black and minority ethnic women (Griffin, 1986; 1993)

One area in which Asian youth did feature was the body of work identified as the ethnicity school. This involved an exploration of ethnic minority community life in Britain in the 1970s (see *inter alia* Khan, 1976). In this literature however, young Asians and Asian girls' experiences in particular, were presented exclusively in ethnic or cultural terms and often with reference to the cultural pathology discourse, which I have shown to be based on the assumption that the 'problems' faced by Asian girls stem inherently from their familial and cultural backgrounds, with the implicit additional assumption that this background is somehow inferior or inadequate when compared with western family structure and society. The Community Relations Commission (CRC) for example, opened their book with the following statement:

> The children of Asian parents born or brought up in Britain are a generation caught between two cultures. They live in a culture of their parents at home, and are taught a different one at school, the neighbourhood, at work ... parents cannot fully understand their children and children cannot fully understand their parents. (CRC1976:1)

The aim of their project was to investigate the nature, causes and consequences of inter-generational conflict within the Asian community and to suggest ways in which the effects of this conflict might be mitigated. They proceeded to argue that Asian children's exposure to British values, norms and attitudes undermined their parents' traditional authority and caused the younger generation to question certain aspects of their parents' culture. Asian girls were said to suffer particularly because of their apparent exposure to conflicting cultures of the home and the wider western society where, it argued, they experienced freedom which was not compatible with their lives at home. John Rex, for example, argued that, 'Asian girls are required to accept considerable limitations to their freedom of movement and above all arranged marriages'. He proceeded to talk about the inevitable breakdown he saw as resulting from the exposure of Asian girls to western culture, particularly in the school:

> There must be few Indian girls who have not been tempted by these possibilities, particularly as they are presented in popular music. Thus being a good Indian, and also being a good middle class student at the same time, are by no means easy goals to attain. There is bound to be breakdown (Rex cited in Lawrence, 1982: 115)

The dominant images found in this literature were of Asian girls 'caught between two cultures' (CRC, 1976; Watson, 1976), with one – western youth culture, represented by the school – 'freer' than the other. Asian girls were also portrayed as the passive victims of static and fixed cultures incapable of change.

In much of this literature, the experiences of Asian girls were presented without reference to a broader social and historical framework that accounts for the subordination of black groups in Britain (Lawrence, 1982; Fryer, 1985; 1988). Instead, essentialist accounts have been made to support static representations of Asian communities as incapable of change. In a wider critique of the ethnicity school or race relations approach, Miles (1982:64) argued that by using ethnicity to refer to the 'perception of group difference', the term was made to refer to any criteria by which a group might distinguish itself from another. Secondly, an exclusive emphasis on culture in the work of the ethnicity school served to conceal the economic, political and ideological conditions that allow the attribution of meaning to take place. The Centre for Contemporary Cultural studies (CCCS) was the other main critic of the ethnicity school tradition, arguing that in the work of the ethnicity school researchers:

> Culture is seen as an autonomous realm which merely 'intersects' with other social processes. The effect of this is to produce a static and idealised vision of Asian cultures, which cannot really take account of class, caste, regional differences and which cannot help us to understand how and why those 'cultures' have changed ... for the ethnicity school studies researchers, the relationship between ethnic minority and ethnic majority society is viewed in exclusively cultural terms. (CCCS, 1981: 113-114)

Asian girls in the literature in the 1980s

As a direct response to such culturalist perspectives, literature in the 1980s and 1990s presented alternative accounts of Asian girls' experiences. In the 1980s, empirical work challenged the negative imagery of Asian girls by situating their accounts within a wider social and historical framework (Amos and Parmar, 1981; Parmar and Mirza, 1983; Brah and Minhas, 1985; Parmar, 1988). In such research, Asian girls reportedly defended themselves from racist attack by forming friendships based on a positive identification as Asian.

Amos and Parmar (1981) for example, in their groundbreaking chapter, argued that the experiences of Asian girls should not be marginalised as a separate issue, but should be an integral feature of writings on sexuality, family life and other aspects of institutional racism which impinge on the lives of black women. They argued that a focus on cultural practices such as arranged marriages shifts blame from racism in wider society and the historical legacy of racism which has shaped the experiences of black groups in Britain:

> ... our cultural norms and values have been seen as responsible for bad housing, overcrowded schools and unemployment, amongst other social ills. By adopting such a perspective, white academics and practitioners in so-called 'helping and caring' professions have shifted the blame from the nature of the society we live in to our religion, culture and communities. (*ibid*:131)

In opposition to such culturalist approaches, Amos and Parmar took as their starting point the racism black communities in Britain experienced, its historical roots in colonialism and its contemporary role in shaping the position and experience of black girls in Britain. They highlighted structural racism in both the labour market and in schools, where Asian girls have experienced racism not only from white teachers but also from white students.

Brah and Minhas (1985) extended this analysis, arguing that colonialism and imperialism have shaped the experiences of black groups in Britain and that schools are not neutral but are a microcosm of society. They argued that Asian girls are thus falsely stereotyped as passive, shy, docile and timid and are often systematically ignored by teachers during classroom interaction unless the question arises of arranged marriages. Asian girls are also stereotyped as smelly and ugly, and perceived as sexual rejects that warrant physical and verbal abuse. Brah and Minhas maintained that the perpetrators justify this sexual and racial harassment by arguing that Asian girls fail to stand up for themselves. Thus they found a 'blaming the victim' effect which supports the findings of Amos and Parmar.

Brah and Minhas also examined the content of the school curriculum which they see as 'eurocentric, explicitly and implicitly racist and sexist and biased against the working class' (1985:23). Their study revealed that Asian girls, given English as a second language (ESL) training, receive a restricted curriculum which effectively bars them from taking certain subjects and has serious implications for their future role in the labour market. Even girls fluent in English are channelled to certain subjects and often the potential outcome of taking such subject combinations is not fully explained to them. More overtly, careers guidance teachers dismiss the aspirations as 'too high'.

This supports the findings of Parmar (1988), who reports on a young Asian woman who approached a teacher for advice being told:

> What's the point of giving you any advice. Stop dreaming and be realistic. You're probably going to be married off anyway so don't waste time educating yourself. (Parmar, 1988:109)

Brah and Minhas observed that groups of Asian girls were conscious of the stereotypes which prevailed and resisted them in a variety of ways. This resistance included pretending not to hear instructions, using their home language as a weapon and forming all Asian girl groups to defend themselves from attack.

As discussed in the next chapter, in the wider literature this resistance response was not fully elaborated and amounted to little more than tokenism (Amos and Parmar, 1981). Therefore, while this work represented an important challenge to ahistorical and essentialist accounts produced within the ethnicity school tradition, its predominant focus on a positive Asian identity meant that divisions or internal struggles among Asians were not fully explored.

Asian girls in the literature in the 1990s
In the 1990s, and against the background of sociological debates on difference and identity, the literature on young Asian women has tended to

focus on specific sub-groups, especially Muslims (Brah, 1993a; Knott and Khoker, 1993; Haw, 1994; Basit, 1997a; 1997b), or Sikhs (Bhachu, 1991; Drury, 1991). More sophisticated analyses have drawn explicitly on historical and political frameworks to examine the active role played by women in the transformations of their local and regional cultures, in changing economic contexts (e.g. Brah, 1993; Bhachu, 1991). Other researchers (especially Drury, 1991; and Basit, 1997a; 1997b) have focused primarily on the distinctiveness of the cultures inhabited by young Sikh women (Drury) and young Muslim women (Basit), without explicit reference to the structural factors that impact differentially on the lives of these young women.

Drury (1991) for example, distinguishes between different ways of conforming to or abandoning Sikh traditions. She found that while some Sikh traditions had been abandoned, the majority were maintained or modified by Sikh girls. Contrary to the ethnicity school's research, there were few signs of overt inter-generational conflict in Drury's research. This was because parents allowed their daughters to abandon some traditions. Drury refers to this as established non-conformity. She also argued that it was possible to identify different categories of maintenance and non-adherence. A distinction could therefore be made between those girls who maintained Sikh traits in deference to parental expectations (unwilling conformity) and those who did so of their own volition (willing conformity). Drury found that some young Sikhs confined certain traditions to specific contexts whilst others maintained them in all situations where traditions had been abandoned (selective conformity). Examples were found both of parental consent and of girls either covertly or overtly disregarding parental wishes. Thus she argues:

> Ethnic cultures do not remain static since members of the first generations can and do sometimes modify or abandon them so as to accommodate changes in their lives in Britain. (1991:387)

In viewing Sikh cultures as dynamic rather than static, Drury's research provides an alternative reading of young Asian women's experiences to that found in the ethnicity school literature. In identifying responses other than resistance it also presents a challenge to the resistance literature (Amos and Parmar, 1981; Parmar, 1988; Brah and Minhas, 1985). However, Drury's primary focus on ethnicity marginalises the constraining role of racism in the lives of young Sikh women. In fact her only reference to racism is contained in the finding that the girls believe that there should be Sikh teachers in schools to challenge the prejudices of white children who 'sneer and laugh at them'. In this sense her approach is much closer to the work of ethnicity school researchers because it lacks an explicit historical and structural perspective; that is, like the ethnicity school researchers, she does not situate Sikh cultures within a wider social and historical context which refers to the systematic subordination of black groups in Britain.

Basit (1997b) examines the role of the family in shaping present experiences and future aspirations of British Muslim adolescent females. Through an analysis of interviews with young women, their teachers and their parents, she explores some of the assumptions that are held by teachers of British Muslim girls. She argues that teachers assume Muslim girls to be restricted within the home and to experience more freedom within the school, but does not account for the origins of such assumptions nor for their impact on the school experience of young Muslim women. She does not question why many teachers share these assumptions, nor why these assumptions are also commonly held of non-Muslim Asian girls, for example Sikhs (see Wise, 1995). Assumptions about young Muslim women are therefore not related to contemporary and historical discourses of Muslim and Asian cultures as 'heathen, backward and barbaric' (Lawrence, 1982; Fryer, 1985; 1988; Brah, 1993), nor located within a wider economic and political framework. There is in the conclusion a brief reference to the changing shape of racisms but this is not explored in the body of the article, which focuses on 'cultural misunderstandings' between the 'majority British population' and British Asian Muslims (*ibid*:426). Indeed it is argued that the solution to these cultural misunderstandings lies in further dialogue between the two groups, who each hold negative stereotypes about the other:

> It is manifest that the process of stereotyping is reciprocal....While there is a need for educators to have an understanding of the social world of the young people they work with and the reason they choose to live their lives in certain ways, there is also a need for ethnic minorities to understand why the notion of freedom is sacrosanct to the majority group. Clearly in order to avoid the perpetuation of stereotypes, more contact and dialogue between the ethnic majority and ethnic minority groups is crucial. (*ibid*: 437)

This solution is itself based on a mistaken assumption of equal power relations between majority and minority groups, about the commitment to engage in full dialogue and also about the effectiveness of dialogue. Consequently there is a lack of acknowledgement of power structures of, for example, gender, race and class, and of how these intersect with the everyday experiences of young Asian women in historically specific periods. Due to this neglect, Basit's analysis fails to account for the complex ways in which Asian girls are defined and how they are able to define and respond differentially to the experiences of schooling in contemporary society. Indeed, the focus on specific subgroups diverts attention from some of commonalities that may exist across groups within the Asian category. In the next section I draw on work of Gramsci (1971) to establish an analytical framework that can account for the ways in which structures – including education – can shape and influence the experiences of Asian girls without necessarily *determining* them. the framework can also account for the commonalities and divisions that may exist within the category *Asian girl.*

Re-theorising the experiences and responses of young Asian women

While Gramsci's work is not specifically concerned with contemporary English society, nor with education as a social institution, his concepts and ideas have been developed and applied by researchers in relation to English society and other contemporary capitalist societies, for example by Hall (1980), Hall *et al* (1978), CCCS (1982). It can also be found in the approaches of Brah (1993a), Anthias and Yuval-Davis (1992), Bhavnani (1993). Hall's reading of Gramsci has also been particularly influential in sociological debates on identity and cultural studies (see Parmar, 1990; Rutherford, 1990; Mani and Frankenberg, 1993).

Gramsci's concepts of *historical specificity, articulation and hegemony* are a persuasive attempt to move beyond the problems of ahistoricism and essentialism found in some of the approaches outlined in the previous section. By historical specificity Gramsci means a particular social formation at a particular point in time; by articulation, he meant the inter-relationship of economic, political and ideological structures in specific historical periods. Gramsci's concept of hegemony allows for the possibility of resistance to limits that are set on experiences. His term hegemony referred to a set of practical assumptions or a worldview that secures the domination of a particular group (ruling bloc) with, in the main, the consent of the subordinated, though co-ercion remains in reserve. Gramsci argued that hegemony is never com-plete. There are always alternative practices and ideas continually emerging, both within and without the dominant hegemony. Some of these initiatives are oppositional or counter-hegemonic and pose a real threat to the social order. Others are incorporated within the basic terms of the dominant meaning system.

Developing the concept of hegemony, Williams (1980) refers to a dis-tinction between *alternative* and *oppositional* cultures, where alter-native cultures are those which coexist with the dominant culture and can be easily tolerated and incorporated into it, whereas oppositional cultures have the potential to be revolutionary and pose a real threat to the dominant culture. This, however, is dependent on the precise social and political forces operating at the time. In contrast to class reduc-tionist approaches, both Gramsci and Williams emphasised the im-portance of forming political alliances based on divisions other than class, in order to seriously challenge the hegemony of a dominant group. These political identities for Gramsci would be the 'first repre-sentations of a new historic phase', 'the nucleus of a new ideological and theoretical complex; what was previously secondary and sub-ordinate, even incidental, is now taken to be primary' (Gramsci, 1971: 195).

The experiences of Asian girls need to be understood within the context of 'articulation', or in the intersection of their every day lives with the economic political relations of subordination and domination (Rutherford, 1990:20). For Gramsci, this articulation is:

> ... the starting point of critical elaboration: it is the consciousness of what one really is, and how 'knowing thyself' as a product of the historical pro-cess to date which deposited an infinity of traces, without leaving an inventory ... each individual is the synthesis not only of existing relations but of the history of these relations he is a precis of the past. (Gramsci, cited by Forgacs, 1988:326)

Applying this understanding to Asian girls' experiences reveals that race, gender, class and age divisions cannot be mechanically added, nor reduced to one or other of the divisions. Instead, these divisions must be seen as interrelated in a complex fashion, and as underpinned by the

simultaneous operation of economic, political and ideological structures in the historical juncture of late twentieth and early twenty first
century Britain (Parmar, 1988). As Parmar has observed:

> A relevant and valid theory for analysing the situation of black women has
> to necessarily base itself on the fact of the simultaneous nature of their
> exploitation and oppression. It would not be useful to dissect these
> different power systems and attempt to strip them away as if they formed
> layers of oppression, because the daily subjective experiences which form
> the matrix of young black women's lives are formed by their fusion.
> (Parmar, 1988: 197)

It is important also to recognise that identities are not fixed but are
relational, complex, differentiated and constantly repositioned. Thus,
Asian girls may be defined and may define themselves in different ways
depending upon the particular time, context and place (Parmar, 1990;
Mani and Frankenberg, 1993; Rutherford, 1990). For example, a
Muslim girl of Pakistani descent living in England may be defined or
define herself by reference to race (as black), religion (as Muslim),
nationality (British) or ethnicity (either Pakistani or Asian), depending
upon the context in which definition takes place.

Historical specificity requires that the position of Asian girls today is
understood within the context of the complex social and historical processes that account for the subordination of black groups in Britain.
Social relations in capitalist patriarchal societies such as Britain are set
against the background of colonialism and imperialism (Brah and
Minhas, 1985: 14-15). It is not simply that colonialism is reproduced
but also that its ideologies are re-worked in the shifting relations of late
modernity and globalisation and are concretely articulated with other
divisions of gender, ethnicity and class (Brah, 1993; Hall, 1992).

The class locations of the families of Asian girls cannot be understood
without reference to this global, social and historical context. Migration
from the former colonies was actively encouraged to help Britain re-
build the economy, following the shortage of labour in the aftermath of
the second world war. As commentators have argued (Amos and
Parmar, 1981; and Fryer, 1988), this migration also resulted from the
systemic economic exploitation and plunder by the British during their
colonial occupation of parts of Asia, Africa and the Caribbean. By comparison with immigrants from the West Indies, Asians and especially

Indians were more likely to be members of the skilled working class or professional and business classes (Bagley, 1969, cited in Taylor, 1985). Large numbers of doctors, engineers, scientists and teachers arrived in Britain with vouchers for the 'special skills' category of the 1962 Immigration Act. In 1965-7, some 2,942 teachers from India and 577 from Pakistan were admitted (Rose et al, 1969). Also recruited were professional and business people from East Africa (Kenya and Uganda).

However, the majority of immigrants from the Indian subcontinent were land labourers and therefore classed as unskilled. They found work predominantly in manufacturing industries (Taylor, 1985). Immigrants from the Indian subcontinent were primarily motivated by the desire to find work. Consequently, they tended to settle in inner cities where employment and housing could be more easily found. This has had a lasting legacy in urban areas (ibid; Garland, 1996). Evidence (Rose et al, 1969; Beckerlegge, 1991) suggests that concentrations of Asian communities are found in particular areas of Britain, and that religion and region of origin have also influenced the development of distinct communities in those areas. Modood (1992) has noted that Pakistani Muslims from the Mirpur region are more likely to be found in high numbers not in London but in industrial towns and cities such as Rochdale, Bradford and Manchester, where they found work in textile mills. So they are located in the areas that have suffered most from economic recession in England. This is supported by figures from the Labour force survey (cited in Labour Market Trends, 1997:300) which show that Pakistanis and Bangladeshis have substantially higher rates of unemployment than other ethnic groups (24% for Pakistani and Bangladeshis, whites 7.9%, black 14%, Indian 12%). For women, these figures are higher (28% Pakistani and Bangladeshi compared with Indian 11%, white 6.1%, and black 17%). Clearly this has implications for the class locations and settlement patterns of Asian girls' families, which in turn affect the type of schooling they receive and ultimately their future qualifications and employment.

Thus young Asian women, like all people, are located in economic contexts that are historically shaped. In the cultural sphere too there are complexities.

Asian girls are subject to prevailing gender regimes in England (Brah and Minhas, 1985). However, they fall outside the stereotypical images which bombard the everyday experiences of white women and girls, though within racialised stereotypes (Parmar, 1988; Connolly, 1998), as argued in chapter one. Currently these images are located in attempts at crisis management that have resulted in the re-activation of racist ideologies. These images are rooted in Britain's imperial past but re-worked in the definition of black groups as a 'problem' that poses a 'threat to the British way of life' (CCCS, 1982; Barker, 1981; Solomos and Back, 1993). The state, through its implementation of immigration control policies since the 1950s in England, has played a central role in the racialisation of immigration; that is, in the identification of im-migration as a black issue and therefore as problematic (Solomos, 1992; Miles, 1993). This racialisation process has produced a number of (sometimes) contradictory discourses on different sections of the black community: African Caribbean men are predominantly associated with criminal activities involving drugs and prostitution; Asian men have been portrayed as equally problematic, though primarily as exploiters of the welfare system. African Caribbean women have been depicted as independent but sexually available. This racial stereotyping has resulted in images of Asian women as dependants who are 'controlled by their men' (WING, 1985; Klug, 1989).

Discourses on black *youth* are also important for understanding Asian girls' schooling and identity. In the last four decades in England these have been contradictory and shifting. Young black men have been com-monly identified as 'problems' but in different ways at different his-torical moments (CCCS, 1982, Gilroy and Lawrence, 1988). In the context of schooling, young African Caribbean men have been con-sistently portrayed as a problem to discipline and as 'underachievers' who are lazy and aggressive (*ibid*, Sewell, 1998). Asian youth by contrast have been portrayed as hardworking and passive but since the late 1980s, particularly in the wake of the Rushdie affair, new dis-courses on Asian masculinity have emerged that position them as volatile, aggressive, angry and hot-headed and as posing a threat to the social order (Searle, 1993; Solomos and Back, 1994), partly because they refuse to accept passive status. These discourses have been further strengthened by the 'riots' in English towns and cities such as Bradford, Burnley, Stoke-on-Trent in 2001 and also in the aftermath of the September 11 attacks on America because they connect with wider dis-courses on Muslims as barbaric and backward.

It is only against this social and historical background that the schooling and identity of Asian girls can be understood. For example, it is the context of the language and imagery invoked by current discourses of black people as undesirable, Muslims as barbaric and backward, and Asian boys and men as volatile, angry and hot-headed, that Asian girls (including those of non-Muslim origin) have been positioned as ever more passive, timid, quiet and shy, as the victims of cultural practices which oppress them.

Such discourses fuel common assumptions in relation to Asian girls' schooling, for example, that they are constrained by cultural requirements to expect arranged marriages. Such assumptions do not take into account the fact that Asian girls' lives are also affected by the gender relations which prevail among the particular Asian group to which they belong. Some young women may indeed be constrained by the gender relations in operation within their families but the cultural-constraints argument mis-represents the home lives of *all* young Asian women. Gender relations vary not only from one group within the Asian category, such as Muslim or Indian, to another but also within particular families across these groups. As well as gender relations, other axes of differentiation need to be taken into account when theorising Asian girls' experiences of schooling and society, such as class position in the English context, religion, language and caste, area of origin, region, sexuality and ability.

We have seen that the areas from which their parents and grandparents have migrated are also varied. Three main religions are practised by Asians in Britain – Islam, Hinduism and Sikhism – at least five languages are spoken – Punjabi, Gujerati, Bengali, Pushto and Urdu – and there are a multitude of castes (Shah, 1992; Taylor, 1985). Young Asian women are also subject to influence from the local and regional cultures in which they are located. These factors combine to produce specific experiences for young Asian women in Britain; Asian cultures in London may be distinguished from their counterparts in Birmingham or those of east London from west London. As Brah (1993a) has pointed out:

> The lived cultures than young Muslim women inhabit are highly differentiated according to such factors as country of origin, rural/urban background prior to migration, regional and linguistic background in the

> subcontinent, class position in the subcontinent as well as in Britain, and regional location in Britain. British Asian cultures are not simply a carry-over from the [country of origin] ... Hence Asian cultures of London may be distinguished from their counterparts in Birmingham. Similarly, east London cultures have distinctive features as compared with those from west London. (Brah, 1993: 448-9)

The experiences of Asian girls are therefore shaped by a multiplicity of factors including race, gender, class, ethnicity, ability, sexuality, regional origin of parents, religion and their regional location in England. While social structures and practices may set limits on the kinds of experiences Asian girls have, they cannot be said to *determine* them. Following Gramsci and Williams, I wish to argue that people are not determined by the conditions in which they find themselves, but rather that there is 'space' in the cultural sphere to resist and challenge dominant definitions. It is in this process of articulation that identities are produced. For Asian girls in England, schooling is the major *public* site for the active negotiation of their identities. The ways in which Asian girls experience or respond to schooling depends not only on the particular configuration of the relationship between the various structural factors that shape their experiences but also on their subjective experiences of the situations in which they find themselves. That is, they are able to position themselves in various ways in relation to dominant cultural definitions of them. According to Davies and Harre (1990:48), *positioning* is:

> the discursive process whereby selves are located in conversations as observably and subjectively coherent participants in jointly produced story lines. There can be interactive positioning in which what one person says positions another. And there can be reflexive positioning in which one person positions oneself.

Central to the process of positioning are current discourses on race, gender, class as they are filtered through popular constructions of Asian femininity. I am interested in both interactive and reflexive position as they impact on the girls' schooling and identity. The ways in which these various positionings have been read by researchers in the academic study of youth and of Asian girls is the subject of the next chapter as I set the context for the discussion of the strategies Asian girls employ to deal with their experiences of schooling and society.

3
Theorising resistance, defence and survival

Various structural factors shape Asian girls' experiences of schooling and society but they do not determine them. In this chapter, I examine some of the ways in which researchers have set about conceptualising or understanding the ways young people make sense of the situations in which they find themselves. I begin by exploring examples of subcultural resistance theory which, influenced by Gramscian concepts, has focused attention on everyday life for signs of class conflict and resistance, but has drawn criticism for employing an all-embracing concept of resistance that cannot account for the complexity of young people's experiences today. In the 1990s in the context of post-modernism and post-structuralism, attention shifted to focus on alternative discourses of defence and survival revealing various coping strategies adopted in identity-making processes. I discuss some of the research specifically addressing Asian girls' strategies against this background. The chapter ends with a brief outline of the research study on which this book draws in order to set the context for Asian girls' strategies discussed in chapters four to seven.

Studies of youth resistance

Since the 1950s researchers have been interested in the ways young people define their experiences and the various strategies they use to deal with these experiences. A classic text is *Resistance through Rituals*, where Hall and Jefferson (1975) focus on the class basis of youth subcultures as a response to the concept of classless youth that began to emerge in the British literature on youth in the 1950s and 1960s (Abrams, 1959; Coleman, 1962). Their analysis is located in the context of economic and social conditions that provided the backdrop

THE SCHOOLING AND IDENTITY OF ASIAN GIRLS

for the definition of youth as a social problem. Hall and Jefferson developed a sophisticated argument that sought to consider the relationship between class and youth within a Gramscian framework. This emphasised the problem of ideology and culture, and taking Marx's dialectical analysis that people are formed and form themselves through culture and history, Hall and Jefferson defined culture as:

> ... [that] level at which groups develop distinct patterns of life and give 'expressive form' to their social and material existence ... Culture is the way the social relations of a group are structured and shaped: but it is also the way those shapes are experienced, understood and interpreted. (1976:11)

Just as groups and classes stand in rank or order to one another so cultures are differently ranked. Cultures do not stand in direct opposition to one another, however; instead they coexist. Drawing on Gramsci (1971), Hall and Jefferson argue that the dominant culture is not completely homogenous, since divisions exist between various sections who can have opposing interests. Its dominance is therefore never complete. There is always space for other cultures to challenge or resist its cultural hegemony. By adopting the concept of hegemony, the power exercised by one social group over another with their consent and with coercion always in reserve, Gramsci drew attention to the role of cultural or civil institutions (such as the church, the family, the law, or education, arts and media) in the organisation of power in class societies. Gramsci argued that for a class to be hegemonic, it must rule in not only the economic sphere (where production is organised) but also the political (police and military) and civil institutions, the way people organise their 'private' lives, and 'common-sense' (the ways in which they each understand their situation and decide what is right and wrong). Thus for Gramsci, class struggle involves the battle for ideas as well as the struggle for state and economic power. It follows that ideological resistance is a key form of political activity. Since hegemony is never complete, there are always challenges to the hegemony of a particular group.

For Hall and Jefferson, deviant youth styles in the form of 'subcultures' present such a challenge. They define the term subculture in terms of its relationship to the parent culture and more widely in terms of its relationship with the dominant culture. Subcultures are 'sub-sets – smaller, more localised and differentiated structures, within one or other of the larger cultural networks' (*ibid*:13). But they are not simply 'ideological constructs':

> Subcultures too, win space for the young: cultural space in the neighbour-hood and institutions, real time for leisure and recreation, actual room on the street or street corner. They serve to mark out and appropriate 'territory' in the localities. They focus around key occasions of social interaction: the weekend, the disco, the bank holiday trip, the night out in the 'centre', and 'stand -about-doing-nothing' of the weekday evening, the Saturday match. (*ibid*: 45-6).

It is this aspect that underpins much of the work drawing on subcultural resistance theory which looks to culture and everyday life for signs of class conflict and resistance – essentially of how people make sense of the situation in which they find themselves.

Willis (1977), for example, also draws on a Gramscian concept of resistance rather than traditional Marxist concepts of cultural reproduction. He identifies a 'space' for the operation of resistant cultures of working class boys rather than assuming that cultures are produced by economic workings of the capitalist system. The working class boys or 'lads' in his study adopt an anti-school stance, which Willis identifies as a counter culture. This counter school culture has parallels with a shop floor culture found in the factory, drawing on oppositional elements from working class culture. Thus some of the strategies centre on the shared focal concerns of 'toughness', 'machismo', 'independence' and 'enjoyment'. The lads in Willis' study reject mainstream values in the school, expressing opposition to authority. Their resistance takes the form of fighting, truancy, lateness, vandalism, smoking and drinking. The lads resent conformists in the school, whom they call 'earoles'.

Willis argues that their cultural background, whilst providing them with the means to resist, at the same time provides the means of enslavement. It is the 'fatalism' which is a key element of working class culture that prevents their turning their symbolic victory into a real one. Thus the lads collude in their own domination by taking an active part in their confinement to factory work, and ultimately in reproducing the subordinate position of the working class as whole. This reproduction is not simple, as in theories of direct reproduction, but involves struggle. Willis argues that social agents are not passive bearers of ideology but active appropriators who reproduce existing structures only through struggle, contestation and partial penetration of those structures (Willis, 1977).

One of the criticisms that Willis' work has attracted is that he accepts 'at face value the lads' view that the conformists in the school cannot, at the same time as being involved in their school work, also take an interest in some of the things that are at the centre of the world of the lads – music, clothes, the opposite sex, drink etc.' (Blackledge and Hunt, 1985:216). Willis is accused therefore of not recognising the variety of subcultures which may exist within the school. A 'conformist' may also have outside interests, and most pupils may fall somewhere in between his two extremes of 'lads' and 'earoles'. Despite this criticism, Willis' ethnographic study has been influential in providing a model on which subsequent sociological research has been based, including recent studies of masculinities in schooling (Mac an Ghaill, 1994).

Mac an Ghaill (1988) draws on Willis' approach to address the resistant strategies of black youth in his study. The young men of African Caribbean origin (the Rasta Heads) and of Asian origin (the Warriors), in his main study, adopted an anti-school stance similar to that found by Willis. To describe the young women's strategies however, Mac an Ghaill draws on Anyon's (1983) concept of 'resistance within accommodation'. This concept also focuses on the resistant strategies of particular oppressed groups to the contradictory situations they find themselves in, but these strategies also involved a degree of accommodation (working within stereotypes to their advantage). Mac and Ghaill (1988) applies this concept to the strategies adopted by a group of young black women to deal their educational experiences in a sixth form college. Those he calls the Black Sisters adopted an anti-school but pro-education approach. This meant that they both accepted and rejected education:

> The Black Sisters, in responding to their schooling in terms of a strategy of resistance within accommodation, provide evidence in the British context to support Anyon's insightful suggestion. On the one hand, they reject the racist curriculum; on the other, they value highly the acquisition of academic qualification. Theirs is a strategy that is both anti school but pro education. (Mac an Ghaill, 1988:11)

In a study of black girls in a London comprehensive school, Fuller (1980; 1982; 1983; see also Wright, 1987) also drew on the concept of resistance within accommodation. She challenged the idea that young black women of African Caribbean origin are 'underachievers' in schools due to poor self-esteem (a claim put forward by theorists conforming to a cultural pathology model in education in the 1970s).

Fuller focused on the experiences of a small number of black girls, arguing that they formed a discernible subculture within the school. This subculture was based on a positive acceptance of their experience of being both black and female. Fuller (1982:92) found that the girls gave every appearance of being 'disaffected' within a classroom context, stating that they saw the school as 'trivial', 'boring' and 'childish'. However, when observed or spoken to outside the school, the testimonies of the girls revealed a deep commitment to achieving educational success. Contrary to the negative self-esteem thesis, the girls had a positive image of their own ability but, because of lack of support and encouragement from parents and male peers, pursued academic qualifications as a public statement of their capability.

In a critique of this research, Mirza (1992) argues that Fuller's concept of 'cultures of resistance' results in an emphasis on subcultural features of youth. This, Mirza argues, has had the effect of diverting attention away from issues which Hall and Jefferson (1976) see as determining the quality of the experiences of those being studied (issues such as unemployment, compulsory mis-education, low pay and dead-end jobs). According to Mirza, Fuller's account:

> ... results in an unrealistic, 'romantic' reappraisal of black girls' actions and decisions. Fuller's belief that these girls were highly politicised about unemployment, racism and sexism during their educational career and planned their actions as a defiant gesture to the world, does not stand up to closer scrutiny. Research by Ullah (1985) indicated that young black women were the least aware of the groups in the study of the racism they would encounter in the work-place. (Mirza, 1992:23)

In relation to African Caribbean women, Mirza argues that it is not enough to show how racist and sexist ideologies are constructed in the consciousness of individuals or groups. Rather, a demonstration is required of how the ideology of sexually structured racism, as a dynamic and politically constructed ideology, maintains disadvantage by its effect on economic assumptions and values. So it is important to investigate the mechanisms of racial discrimination beyond a mere discussion of the dominant ideology and the subsequent creation of cultures of resistance and to include an explanation of its operation through various agencies, such as the school, careers service, youth schemes and other institutions. Mirza sets out to do just this in her study of young African-Caribbean women's experiences of schooling and the discrimination in the labour market.

Subcultural resistance theories have also been criticised more widely (see Gewirtz, 1991:189-90) because they do not always operate clear criteria for distinguishing between behaviour which is resistant and that which is merely 'messing about'. Gewirtz draws for example on Giroux's distinction between 'forms of oppositional behaviour that can be used for either the amelioration of human life or for the destruction and denigration of basic human values'. For Giroux, 'only the former category should be regarded as resistance'. Accordingly, he argues that resistance involves a commitment to 'freedom and emancipation' and to the 'struggle against domination and submission' (Giroux, 1983:289).

A second problem in this body of work is that *what* is being resisted is not always clearly established. Gewirtz takes issue with Mac an Ghaill's interpretation of the demotion of members of the Rasta Heads from the top stream as evidence that they have rejected competitive individualism. She argues that that this seems rather a large jump, maintaining that Anyon's deduction that tomboyishness represents a resistance to stereotyped femininity is a logical step, as is her observation that girls may use displays of 'girlish' behaviour and overt sexuality in order to disrupt lessons and even demonstrate resistance. However, it is difficult to understand how tomboyish behaviour and conforming to expectations of feminine behaviour are examples of rejection of norms of femininity (Gewirtz, 1991:90; see also Hargreaves, 1982).

A further problem is that resistance theories (except Anyon's) focus predominantly on the behaviour of working class pupils. This implies that middle class pupils either do not experience sexism or racism, or that unlike their working class counterparts they internalise dominant ideologies unproblematically. As we have seen, Blackledge and Hunt (1985) single out Willis for criticism for ignoring the variety of subcultures that exist in a school.

Discourses of defence and survival

During the 1980s, a shift occurred in radical youth research away from the discourse of resistance to discourses of defence and survival. Griffin (1993:146-50, 193-5) sees this shift as situated in the wider economic and political conditions of high unemployment and of 'riots' in the era of Thatcherism in Britain and Reaganism in America. These changes were paralleled by a crisis in sociological thought.

> The events of the late 1970s and early 80s threw radical youth subcultural research into some disarray, highlighting the disjuncture between the structural arguments of cultural Marxism and the growing force of post-modern and post-structuralist ideas, as well as the influence of radical black Marxist/feminist researchers. (Griffin, 1993:147)

Against this background there was growing reluctance to read off the meanings and political implications of specific youth cultural forms as either resistant or conformist. Discourses of resistance became more reflexive in the mid 1980s. In the late 1980s, research on football hooliganism (Haynes, 1992; Redhead, 1991) reported white working class youth as 'beleaguered by the social and economic conditions in Thatcher's Britain, harsh policing strategies and a new dehumanising treatment in popular press' (Griffin *ibid*:149).

These developments have been paralleled in feminist literature of youth where researchers have avoided the discourse of resistance in favour of discussions of the negotiations and strategies (Beuret and Makings, 1989) or of defence and survival (Roberts, 1986; Lowman, 1989). In the feminist literature on sexual abuse and harassment, young women were presented as capable of adopting strategies of resistance, coping and/or survival (see Halston, 1989). Other radical analyses addressed the debate over the relationships between structure, culture and agency, and between subjects and texts (Willis, 1990; Griffin, 1993:194-5).

It is against this theoretical and wider economic and political background that we can locate studies on Asian girls' responses to the situations in which they find themselves.

Research on Asian girls – from the politics of resistance to identity politics

One of the earliest commentaries on Asian girls' resistance/experiences of dealing with their social situations came from Sue Sharp (1976), who devoted one chapter to black girls' experiences in a wider study of girls' schooling in Ealing, London. She found that the Asian girls in her study, who were predominantly Indian and East African, resisted the stereotypes of meekness and submissiveness by disobeying their parents and having relationships with the opposite sex :

> Girls who have been to school in Britain and have adopted some of our beliefs and values are beginning to resist their traditional Asian role and are seeking more freedoms: such as freedom to determine aspects of their own lives like marriage, and freedom to sell their labour in jobs of their choosing. Asian girls in Britain are looking forward to the prospect of greater autonomy and choice than they have had before or would have at home. But the processes of change and the intricacies of female liberation involve complexities that can perhaps be helped by a better understanding of both their predicament and our own. (1976: 298)

Sharp's conclusions concur with those of the ethnicity school literature discussed in chapter two, in that she associates British values and beliefs with freedom, but unlike the ethnicity school researchers, she attributes a more active role to the girls in seeking these freedoms. They are thus not constructed as passive.

The main body of literature addressing Asian girls' resistant strategies in the 1980s was not about their lack of autonomy but centred on their experiences of sexism and class discrimination in mainstream British society as this was filtered through racism. They therefore located the experiences of Asian girls in the social and historical framework that accounts for the subordination of black groups. Much of this literature (Amos and Parmar, 1981, Parmar and Mirza, 1981, Parmar, 1988, Brah and Minhas, 1985) set about challenging not only the invisibility of Asian girls in much of the youth literature but also the negative imagery of Asian girls that was found in the ethnicity literature and wider society.

Brah and Minhas (1985) and Parmar (1988), for example, identified racism as the key factor shaping the experiences of Asian girls. This meant that dominant stereotypes of white femininity could not be applied directly to Asian girls whose experiences of school were filtered through the lens of racism. Unlike white girls, Asian girls were sexual others – that is they were considered to be sexual rejects because of their ethnic background. They were therefore stereotyped as smelly and ugly and often subjected to both verbal and physical abuse. Parmar (1988) discovered common experiences, perceptions and situations which create a strong and uniting bond amongst Asian women. The girls in her study resisted verbal and physical attack by forming all-Asian girl groups based upon a positive experience of being Asian. One of the consequences of their organising against racist attack was that they were further subjected to name-calling, jeering and taunts from white youth of both sexes because they chose to form these groups.

Brah and Minhas (1985) also found evidence of resistance among Asian girls involving the use of home languages as a weapon of resistance, the pretence of not understanding instructions from teachers and false assertions of the religious significance of jewellery. These were some of the strategies employed by first generation Asian women in the work-place, most notably at the Grunwick, Imperial and Chix plants. Al-though this work-place resistance is now well documented (Wilson, 1978; Parmar, 1982; Brah, 1996), these resistant strategies were not elaborated further in the literature in relation to Asian girls.

The concept of resistance was, however, used in other ways to con-ceptualise the experiences of Asian girls. Against the background of debates on identity influenced by post-modern and post-structuralist theorising, and the increasing focus of youth research on musical and cultural expression as sites of resistance, Hargreaves (1990) focuses not on racism but a lack of autonomy that Asian girls experience due to uneven gender relations within their communities. She sees bhangra as the main vehicle for the expression of this resistance but argues that bhangra discos also provide a context for unity and difference.

Hargreaves characterises bhangra as an example of how the focus on the body links to other features of identity and dimensions of the social totality. Bhangra is a fusion of traditional Punjabi music and dance style with modern beats, which gained popularity during the 1980s after the first English gig in 1981. In 1991, bhangra discos were a regular feature of nightlife in major cities in Britain. Asian youth of all nationalities, religions, and castes attend the discos. In Hargreaves' view, bhangra discos can thus be viewed as the context for both unity and difference. They are a form of cultural expression specific to the young Asian com-munity. She argues:

> Young people express solidarity through subcultures which reflect wider issues such as common histories, social class backgrounds, ages, ethnicity, sexualities and political affiliations. There is a dialectical relationship between the language of the body in dance subcultures and wider historical and social forces. (Hargreaves, 1990:151)

Hargreaves highlights the male control and domination of bhangra discos. Purely in terms of attendance, men outnumber women by three to one, and although the majority of professional dancers are female, they are closely guarded and protected by men. The discos themselves are the sites, often involving violence, for working out gender identities. Men – whether brothers or lovers – seek to establish their manhood by fighting for women or defending their honour. Simultaneously the discos are the site of expression of female resistance to patriarchal structures in the Asian community since, as she points out, the girls and women who do attend are usually there without parental permission (*ibid*:159). Hargreaves thus sees them as expressing resistance to their more general lack of autonomy.

> The growing resistance among Asian women to their lack of autonomy is a result of uneven gender divisions and the growth gender conflict in Asian communities. Gender identities like other identities are the result of struggles and contradictions and are constantly changing. (Hargreaves, 1990:159)

The focus on resistance to their lack of autonomy was taken further by the Women against Fundamentalism (WAF) group in the early 1990s but this time with reference to the role of religion in the lives of young women. In the early 1990s they reported growing resistance to the oppressive role which religious fundamentalism has on many young women's lives. Siddiqui (1991) describes her own experiences as a Muslim girl growing up in Britain and gives us an example of the restrictions placed upon her by dress codes. As we saw in chapter One, these arguments have been extended to organised protest against what they perceive as religious oppression. However, the predominant focus on Islam led to criticisms from scholars such as Modood (1992). By their own admission, WAF have focused predominantly on Muslim fundamentalism but argue that their position against Islam stems from their opposition to the central aim which they identify to be at the heart of the fundamentalist agenda, the control of women's minds and bodies through the policing of their sexualities (Connolly, 1991:73).

Alternatives to resistance

Such arguments were countered in existing and new literature focusing on the positive acceptance of religion among Asian girls. In research that moved away from the concept of resistance to processes of identity formation, Shaw (1988), Mirza (1989) and Knott and Khokher (1993), all with reference to Islam, placed emphasis on religion as the main vehicle for the expression of Asian girls' identities. They challenge the ethnicity school assumption that Asian girls are victims of oppressive religions. Instead, they argue that Islam can provide a positive way forward for Muslim girls. Shaw (1988:165-6) found that her interviewees criticised outsiders' views of their religious beliefs. They challenged the popular misconception that Islam does not allow women to be educated, by providing evidence to the contrary from religious teachings and pointing to the high numbers of Muslim women in education in Pakistani cities.

Mirza (1989), in a study of ten Muslim girls in Bradford, argued that young Muslims made distinctions between religious teachings and cultural interpretations of Islamic teachings (1989:7). The girls were clearly able to distinguish between Islamic teachings from the Quoran and cultural interpretations of Islam prevalent in their communities. Mirza found a new process of identification in which the young women saw themselves as 'Muslim/British' rather than Pakistani/Muslim – an identification that was due to their experiences of living in a different cultural context from their parents. Common links with other Muslims reinforced a desire to retain affiliation with the forces of Islam.

Drury (1991) has also established an alternative to the resistance approaches discussed above, examining the maintenance of some aspects of an ethnic culture by young Sikh women in Nottingham. She adopts a 'situation ethnicity' approach and is influenced by the writings of Barth (1969), according to which the significance of ethnicity depends upon 'an actor's perception of a particular situation, the opportunities, resources and constraints existing within and outside her/his ethnic community and the variability and flexibility of social boundaries between ethnic groups'.

Drury (1991) has favoured the concepts of conformity and non-conformity in her research on Sikh girls and the maintenance of Sikh cultural traditions. This enables her to include responses such as established non-conformity, where parental permission is given for the abandoning of certain norms, and breakaway non-conformity where girls cut their hair, ate meat and deliberately disobeyed religious and cultural requirements regarding the non-consumption of alcohol and cigarettes. She also distinguishes between willing and unwilling conformity and selective conformity (conformity in certain circumstances). This enables her to identify a number of possible responses on the part of Sikh girls rather than an all embracing cultural resistance response found in the earlier research studies on Asian girls. The main problem with Drury's approach is that her focus on ethnicity diverts attention from the racism and the broader socio-historical context that shape Asian girls' experiences.

In my own research, this socio-historical context is crucial to understanding the economic locations of the girls' families and the cultural spaces they inhabit. In this respect I agree with the approach taken in early resistance studies on Asian girls (Brah and Minhas, 1985; Parmar, 1988). I also found evidence of Asian girls adopting a strategy of resistance based on a common experience of being Asian; but there existed other strategies, too, that reflect the ways in which Asian girls are both positioned and position themselves differently in relation to dominant discourses in schooling.

Strategies of resistance and survival in the research study

The following four chapters draw on research completed for my doctoral thesis. The main focus of the research was the strategies employed by a group of Asian girls to deal with their experiences of schooling and society. The girls were aged 13-16 and were sampled across eight schools in the Greater Manchester and Staffordshire areas of England. I conducted semi-structured interviews with 44 girls all of whom were British born, of Pakistani, Bangladeshi or Indian descent and from one of three religious backgrounds, Muslim, Sikh or Hindu.

The girls' families originated from urban/rural backgrounds that may have given rise to different class positions in their country or region of origin but in the English context they were predominantly from working class backgrounds. They were located in economically deprived areas that had suffered from the decline of manufacturing industries. The majority of parents were either unemployed or in low-skilled work. Only three mothers were employed in semi-professional work – two were adult literacy teachers and one was a part-time nurse. The majority (31) were housewives or home workers (five). Of the fathers, one was an engineer, another a building contractor and one a work study analyst but 17 were unemployed (see Appendix 1, table 1). The settlement patterns of the families of Asian girls are shaped by economic processes that encouraged migration from the commonwealth and in turn these settlement patterns influence the type of schooling that Asian girls receive. In this respect the girls are subject to the common class and regionally specific forces that impact as much on the lives of white British girls as they do on Asian girls, but Asian girls' experiences are filtered also through the experience of racism.

The schools the girls attended all contained varied but sizable Asian populations but Pakistani Muslims were in the majority and this is reflected in the research sample (see Appendix 1, table 3). Seven of the eight schools were mixed comprehensives and one was a single sex school, but all contained above average numbers of students who were eligible for free schools meals, a further indication of the low socio-economic status that was a common factor among the girls. So the girls had common 'objective' locations in class, race and regional terms, but the intersection of these structural factors with the girls' subjective experiences in their local situations produced different coping strategies. The categories that I outline over the next four chapters describe these strategies or responses but are not exhaustive or static; they serve instead as a heuristic device to illuminate the complexity of the experiences of Asian girls. These strategies are also historically specific – that is, subject to change so that one girl may employ different responses at different times.

The main strategies fall into four main categories:

Resistance through culture
The 'Gang girls' as I call them, drew on a strategy of 'us and them' like that found in Willis's (1977) study but, unlike his lads, the resistors defined their experiences primarily with reference to racism and positively asserted their identities as Asian.

Survival.
The 'Survivors' adopted a strategy of apparent passivity – working within stereotypes and focusing mainly on achieving academic success

in the long term. They prioritised neither racism nor sexism, though they experienced both.

Rebellion (against culture)

The 'Rebels', as teachers referred to them, prioritised uneven gender relations within their communities. Without actively resisting these, they were critical of parental and community values and they actively dissociated themselves from the Gang girls.

Religious prioritisation

The 'Faith girls', as I call them, adopted a survival strategy and for the most part worked hard to achieve academic success. But they positively asserted their religious identities and were prepared to act defiantly when a religious principle was perceived as being attacked.

A fifth strategy – **Resistance against culture** – was in evidence in pilot work but not in the main study. I mention it here because it does exist even if it is less common. The main characteristics of this response were: western values and tastes being preferred to the traditional cultures of the home; a preference for white students as friends; active resistance against religious and cultural values; the prioritisation of sexism as a source of oppression in the traditional parent communities, in some cases to the denial of racism; identification of themselves as distinct from other Asian students because of their willingness to mix across ethnic groups; identifying racism as caused by the behaviour of black groups themselves (for example, refusal to integrate). Many of these characteristics are similar to those of Rebellion but there are three main differences between the two categories: the Rebels were not prepared to actively resist their parental or cultural practices; they also spoke positively about their familial and community experiences despite being critical of these; and they did not deny the experience of racism, which was a major characteristic of the resistance against culture category.

The reasons for the lack of visibility in the main fieldwork study of resistance against culture are as follows:

First, many of the girls were not interested in resisting their parental cultures because they viewed them as a positive source of identity, as in the resistance through culture category, and/or because they required their parents' trust in order to achieve their academic goals, as in the survival category. Secondly, overt or direct resistance against parental cultures was unnecessary. Some of the girls – primarily the Rebels – were given permission to adapt cultural practices as appropriate. This included such activities as going to night-clubs, associating with the opposite sex, wearing skirts, or any other activities which may usually be unacceptable within the limits set by their particular cultures. A third reason was that the girls, who were not happy with their parental cultures, had learned from the experiences of others that resistance did not pay. Several of them commented about the severe consequences that were possible, such as being withdrawn from school or even being 'sent back to Pakistan'.

In relation to the strategies, fourteen girls could be categorised as Resistors, twelve as Survivors, eight as Rebels and a further eight as Faith girls. Of the forty four girls in the sample, two drew on a combination of resistance and rebellion (see Appendix 2).

As the next four chapters reveal, contrary to the dominant discourse of Asian femininity which constructs them as the passive recipients of oppressive cultural practices, Asian girls were actively engaged in making choices that were influenced by the multiplicity of factors outlined in the previous chapter. These choices informed the conscious strategies they employed to deal with their everyday experiences in school. Each of the next four chapters is organised around a set of themes that emerged from the data and each concludes with a brief discussion of the consequences for schooling of the girls adopting that particular strategy.

4
The Gang Girls

In his study of working class boys or 'lads', Willis (1977) describes the emergence of an 'us and them' culture which ran counter to the school's official culture. The girls in the first of my categories – the 'Gang girls' – also adopted an 'us and them' approach to schooling, but unlike the lads, their experiences were defined primarily with reference to racism and they positively asserted their identities as Asian. The fourteen girls in this category were positioned and positioned themselves in opposition to the dominant culture of the school, which they defined as white and racist.

> [This school's] not that good...the teachers, some of them are racist. They don't treat you that good and some of the children here, they don't treat you that well either. The whites and that, they're really stuck up. (NN)

Often, though not always, this led to the marginalisation of other factors such as gender and class. It was the experience of racism in the school that led to the formation of an all-Asian female subculture from which white students and teachers and Asian students who appeared to ally with whites in the school were excluded. This earned them the label of an Asian gang.

The experience of racism and racist name-calling

Research evidence on the relationships between children within classrooms has shown that victimisation is a common experience for many Asian pupils. Racist name-calling and attacks (Troyna, 1987; Wright, 1992) from white peers are regular daily experiences (Connolly, 1998). The majority of the girls in my study were subjected to some form of verbal abuse, but racist name-calling was experienced most of all by these girls, who were in the lower sets and who chose all-Asian friendships and spoke their home language in the school.

Nine of the girls reported experiencing some form of racial abuse in school. Common insults included, 'Paki' ,' black bitch' , 'black bastard', 'go back to your own country'. The overwhelming majority of girls in the sample made some reference to racist name-calling but these were the girls most likely actively to resist it. Resistance was both individual and collective within the context of the female friendship group and included both verbal and physical forms.

> I just swear back ... [laughs].Well you know they call me 'black bitch' and I just call them 'white bastard'. (YA)
>
> Yeah I've been called things like because of my colour. 'Paki', 'black bitch', I don't care. I just turn around and call them back. I was born in this country and I'll stay in it. (TH)
>
> This boy called me a 'Paki' but I got him back. I called him white 'B'. If someone calls me I call them back. If they want to have a fight. I'll have a fight. (PA)

These comments reveal practices of 'sexual othering' (Brah and Minhas, 1985; Connolly, 1998) in Asian girls' experiences of schooling. Because the girls did not passively accept racism and were prepared to defend themselves, they fell outside the dominant stereotypes associated with both white and Asian femininity. Boys were prepared to attack them physically, including punching and kicking them. The girls' willingness to fight back further reinforced their status as deserving of abuse and characterisations of them as volatile, which are more in line with current discourses on Asian masculinity reviewed in earlier chapters than with femininity.

The girls also made reference to violent incidents in their schools, such as the following, which reveal the materialisation of wider tensions in society.

> FS: Do people get called names often?
>
> YA: Yeah a lot.. There's also violence here...
>
> FS: ....What kind of violence?
>
> YA: Fighting..and sometimes they have to call the police to school every day because there's always fighting – Muslims against English people
>
> FS: How does it all start?
>
> YA: I don't know like cos of the cricket. If Pakistan win then the English get angry and start saying Pakistan are rubbish but the other Pakistanis

can't just shut up, they have to start saying things back and that's how it all starts.

FS: What happens when the cricket's not on? Does it disappear?

YA: It's still there. People who have left this school they come up and start fighting.

FS: White students...?

YA: White students yeah

FS: Have you ever seen anything..?

YA: Yeah, I've seen a lot...Yeah really bad. They get sticks and everything, baseball bats, sometimes they have knives

FS: Really?

YA: Yeah

FS: Have you seen violence?

YA: Yeah?

FS: Can you describe... anyone you know involved?

YA: My brother has – he didn't get hit or anything, but others did, his friends, he just stood on one side and the others...he knew there was a lot of them they would get battered – the others got kicked in the face, nosebleeds

FS: What did the school do?

YA: School doesn't do nothing. A social worker comes round your house and tells us what's going on in the school...

FS: ...your parents...?

YA: ...my mum just lets him come in and wants to talk to him about how the school is bad or anything

Teachers

Teacher-student relations were instrumental in influencing the attitudes of the girls towards their education. While teachers referred to this group as 'trouble-makers' or a gang of Asian girls, the girls spoke negatively about their relationships with teachers. Five of them categorically identified teachers as 'racist' and another six made references to the differential or unfair treatment of them compared with their white peers. Only one of the fourteen girls did not speak directly about teachers as being racist or unfair. The majority commented on the various types of behaviour which they perceived as racist but their perceptions as to what constituted racism differed. Here, systematic neglect by teachers is defined as racist:

> Some of them are okay but some do act racist to us at times like if you go up to them and ask about something they kind of ignore you and talk to the white person first. (HB)

Research (Wright, 1992; Connolly, 1998) has shown that it is a common experience for Asian girls to be ignored or marginalised in classroom interaction because it is assumed that they are industrious, hardworking and get on quietly with their work. The girls in this category, however, were highly visible both in classroom interaction and outside the classroom, where they were often targeted for racial abuse or discrimination. What particularly marked them out from other Asian girls in the school was their determination to oppose such abuse or discrimination. This is evident in the response below, where an Asian girls retells an incident that occurred during a PE lesson:

> PA: I don't like games that much. I like rounders, tennis and cricket, but I don't like the teacher, she's racist, ... she doesn't like Muslims that much. She gives us detention for no reason. I don't know really that much about her, but I've got a friend in the second year and when she was in the first year she [was fasting] right, and she said she wasn't doing games but she didn't bring in a note and she made her do it. And once she put like all the whites on one side and the blacks on one side and she gave the whites shiny green bibs and she said shiny greens versus blacks... When she told me I said, 'what did you do about it?', and she said 'nothing', I said, 'you should have gone to the headmaster and complained', but she said, 'it's too late now '. I said, 'if I were you I would have walked out of the lesson'. It's all right if you do something [wrong], but being racist is just stupid.
>
> F S: What would you have done?
>
> PA: I'd just get out like. I'd talk for my religion, get out and go to the headmaster and ask him what is he going to do about it? What's he going to say to the teacher because she can't do that much about our religion. If she puts whites on one side and blacks on the other then it's not fair is it? If she had mixed them and then given black bibs, it would be okay, but she put blacks on one side.

Whether this happened exactly like this is of less significance than the way in which the girls choose to define the situation and formulate a response to it. While her friend chose to ignore it, PA made an issue of it. This demonstrates her determination to deal with it. This strategy of dealing directly with incidents they perceived as racist was what marked out the Gang girls for further abuse in the school, abuse about which their teachers, in their view, did nothing and which labelled the girls as troublemakers. This led to a lack of trust of the mainstream teachers in the school.

Asian teachers

Only one of the Gang girls said she would approach a white teacher if she had a personal problem. Most highlighted the absence or marginalisation of Asian teachers in mainstream subjects and nine of the fourteen stated that they would prefer to see more Asian teachers in their schools. Although the reasons for wanting Asian teachers varied, there was a general expectation from these students that Asian teachers would or should be 'on their side' or sympathetic to their needs above their duties to the school in general, because of a shared ethnicity:

> By them learning us properly and treating us the same way. (NN)
>
> They can help us with our work more, not all the teachers help. (ZB)
>
> At least they understand your feelings. (NP)

These comments illustrate the girls' feelings of being misunderstood by mainstream teachers in their schools so that Asian teachers seemed to be the solution. Three of the girls did not say whether they wanted more Asian teachers and only two of the fourteen said they would not wish to see more Asian teachers in the school. In both cases the determining factor was not teaching ability but loyalty. The girls expected Asian teachers to express loyalty to them. When they failed to meet these expectations they were reported to have lost sight of their ethnic roots, becoming incorporated (Williams, 1973) instead into the school's official dominant white culture:

> The black teachers, they try to mix in with the white ones and try to become like them. (TH)

TH (labelled a persistent truant by teachers in her school) thus expressed her disappointment with Asian teachers. In her view, these teachers were 'used' by and eventually 'sided with' white authority figures (welfare officers) against her family, warning them that her continued absence from school put them at risk of potential involvement of social services. She had expected her Asian teachers to identify with and be sympathetic to the needs of Asian children and their families, over and above their responsibility to the school. Clearly however, these teachers can have their own priorities and agendas. The idea that Asian teachers should be expected to speak on behalf of their communities reveals a 'burden of representation' (Parmar, cited in Open University, 1993) that is problematic, since Asians are not internally unified and may stand in contradictory or even oppositional positions within their communities. It is not just the Asian girls who place such expectations on Asian teachers; often black teachers generally are expected to have extra skills of communicating about or being the voice of 'their' communities. As Parmar has noted about the parallel position of black artists and film makers:

> There's also this idea of the burden of representation that many of us black artists or film makers or writers are put under, and the problem with that is, there is always this expectation that somehow you are going to be a spokesperson for the Asian community, and I'm always concerned to say that I'm not a spokesperson for the Asian community. Nor is my project about creating or being the voice of Asian women in Britain... People are very eager not to see that our communities are heterogeneous, that we don't come from homogenous communities and that often within our communities, we have different priorities, different agendas. (Parmar, 1993)

For the girls in this category, racism was a defining feature of their school experience and it was this that generated these expectations of Asian teachers and other students in the school. It also provided a vehicle for the expression of their identities in the school context, of which dress and language were important visible markers.

Dress
The majority of the Gang girls wore traditional Asian dress or some modification of their uniform to cultural requirements – where allowed by their school. Ten of the girls explicitly stated a preference for Asian clothes and none expressed preference for western dress.

> I just feel horrible wearing jeans. I don't like going outside without a *dubatta* [head-scarf] on my head. (YA)

There is no way of knowing whether this was an active choice or a justification, but wearing traditional clothes certainly had a significant impact on the girls' experiences of schooling. They visibly stood out as different but chose to articulate a defence of their traditional dress. Thus dress was an important feature in asserting their identities as Asian.

The girls made conscious decisions to defend their traditional outfits and to assert their preference for them. Wearing traditional clothing encouraged and enabled them to identify positively with other girls in similar attire. However, it was also one of the factors which marked them out for racist name-calling in the school because it was read against the schools' dominant white culture as a 'refusal to integrate'. Because the girls defended their traditional dress it became an important site for the contestation of school identities.

Language

Like dress, language was an important vehicle for expressing their identities. Eight girls admitted deliberately using their home language at school to exclude other groups from their conversation, thus using language as a mechanism for excluding white people in school:

> It's great having your own language. It means you say things about them (white students) without them knowing about it (NN)
>
> I speak [my language] at school sometimes with friends .. like when you want to say something and you don't want others to know like when there's Christian people present .. They say speak in our language .. We [say], 'No, we're not saying anything about you, it's just our culture.' [Laughs] English people speak English, Asian people speak their own language. (TH)

Speaking her home language not only marked out a separate Asian identity by excluding white students, teachers and some Asian students who refused to speak their home languages in school, but it also helped to deal with the daily experience of racism by giving the girls a sense of power over the students and teachers they identified as routinely subjecting them to abuse. Further, it helped them to 'win space' as a way of defeating boredom and the low expectations associated with life in the lower sets where the girls were predominately found. School for these girls, as we will see, was therefore viewed as a place merely to have fun and meet friends, because they did not expect to study beyond compulsory schooling.

Academic progress and future career plans

Whatever students' ethnic or religious background, the expectations of them held by teachers can have powerful consequences for their career paths. Wright notes that:

> Teachers expect pupils of Asian origin to be industrious, courteous and keen to learn. They also tend to assume that Asians are well disciplined, highly motivated children from family backgrounds where educational success is highly valued. (1992:39)

The girls did not conform to this ideal of Asian studiousness. Only three were in the mid to higher sets; all the rest were in the lower sets. Most had some idea of the careers they wished to pursue, although as we shall see their actual expectations are lower than their aspirations. Among the careers to which the girls aspired were 'a pilot', 'medicine', 'a vet', 'an air hostess', 'a teacher, nurse or accountant' or 'just working in a shop'. In terms of further and higher education only three of the girls definitely expected to go to college. Two said that their parents 'might' let them proceed and one was not interested. Others had not discussed the issue with their parents.

At first sight their expectations for future academic study appeared to support the stereotypical imagery found in current media discourses that Asian parents do not wish or allow their daughters to be educated beyond secondary school.

> My Mum would let me go on [to Further Education], but my Dad wouldn't, he says, Pakistani girls don't go on. (KB)
>
> My parents are okay but my mum won't let me go on because there [are too many] Asian boys there and English boys and my mum thinks I might get mixed up into [..] wrong things. (YA)
>
> I won't go to college. My father's strict. Some Muslims are spoilt around our area. They all mess around with guys. (NB)

On closer examination however, the responses reveal a more complex picture. The girls themselves talked about the different and often complicated reasons for why parents feel their daughters should not proceed to further and higher studies. An important factor cited by these girls was the fear parents had about their daughters' associating with boys instead of concentrating on their studies. Stories of girls behaving badly and getting mixed up with boys were offered as another reason for parents' reluctance to allow them to proceed into further education.

However, the girls' responses also suggested that the parents' reluctance about further education could sometimes be explained by the behaviour of the girls themselves, or due to negative reports received from the school. Staff who believed that her parents prevented her from pursuing in further education identified TH as bright but a truant, for example. TH herself was in no doubt as to the reason why her parents would not allow her to proceed to further education:

> FS: Why won't your parents let you go onto college?
>
> TH: I mess around too much. I used to truant but now I've stopped.

Her response not only challenges the image of the passive, rule-abiding Asian girl but also illustrates that parents' decisions about their daughters' education may be influenced by the active choices made by the girls themselves – in this case to truant – rather than by the 'cultural constraints' identified in the cultural pathology literature.

It emerged from girls' responses that parents required reassurance from the school that allowing their daughters to proceed to further education would be rewarded by their academic success. If the schools could not assure them that their daughters were capable of studying for advanced level subjects at further education level, parents either withdrew their permission or refused to entertain the idea.

> I thought I was doing well and wanted to go onto to do A levels, but my teacher told my parents that I could do ceramics at college. My parents were really angry and said I couldn't go to college. I'll never forgive him. Until then my parents were happy to for me to go on to college. But now they won't let me. (YA)

It is clear that the view that parents will not allow girls to study further because of cultural constraints is simplistic. Parents' reactions can depend upon the feedback from the school about their child's ability. So if low expectations are communicated to parents, as in the incident cited above, this can have serious consequences for the future career or academic prospects of Asian girls.

Seven of the girls claimed not to have spoken at school about their career aspirations and only one had been interviewed by a careers officer. Significantly, none claimed to have been encouraged in any way by their school.

Friendship patterns
The Gang girls were characterised by their all-Asian female friendship groups, to the exclusion of boys (both white and Asian) and white students generally. The Gang girls viewed such students as 'stuck up'

and avoided them. Eleven of the girls preferred Asian females as friends while three chose a wider mix. Significantly none chose only white girls, and this marked them out from the other groups. Their reasons for choosing Asian friends varied. One was conformity to peer group pressure:

> I mix with Asian people. At my last school I used to mix with Christian people but then I stopped, well people talked. They said I was always mixing with the English and it wasn't right, so I stopped. (TH)

This indicates the strength of peer group pressure on girls. Wright (1992:32) argues that children in her primary study were showing a preference at an early age for members of their own racial/ethnic group and a desire to mix and play only with them. This 'own group' preference did on occasion reflect antipathy towards children of other skin colour or culture. This attitude is evident in one young woman's explanation of why she avoids 'the English':

> HB: They seem dead big-headed to me... I mean it's the way they talk and look down on Asians. The way we dress and the things we eat. Like on Eid or stuff like that. If you start talking about your religion, they think you're some sort of 'tippy'.
>
> FS: What's a tippy?
>
> HB: A typical Pakistani. I'm not being racist or anything but I just don't have anything in common with them [white students] and I just basically don't want to mix with them to tell you the truth.

HB's comments reveal the operation of the cultural pathology discourse in schooling, where the familial and cultural practices of Asians are regarded as inferior to western practices and norms. Rather than internalising this racist discourse, the Gang girls chose to actively dissociate themselves from white students. This engaged them in a struggle to assert the hegemony of their feminine identities in the face of competition from others including the other groups discussed in later chapters. They mixed with their 'own kind' also for security, friendship and empathy:

> I hang out with mainly Asian girls because they know your feelings, like you can know my feelings because you're the same. I think that's why. (NP)
>
> I mix with Pakistanis – they understand my ways. (PD)

An important reason for this choice, however, was the shield from verbal and physical abuse that Asian girl gangs were seen to provide.

> I don't like the English because one time they be's your friend and next time they don't but Pakistanis stick with and don't bully you. (KB)
>
> A lot of Asians because the English don't treat us very well. They just *ignore us* and *batter us*. I used to hang around with English people but Asians understand better. (NN, my emphasis)

The apparent contradiction here is interesting. As with teacher-student relations, the girls' experiences seem to suggest that they are ignored altogether or actively targeted for racial abuse. It is in this context that the all-Asian female network should be read as central to the emergence of an Asian femininity that is produced through their active negotiation with the conditions of their oppression.

This also supports the research evidence of Brah and Minhas (1985), which suggested that the formation of all-Asian girl groups was a mechanism to avoid attack and abuse within the school, but that this group, whether wittingly or unwittingly, became involved in activities which ran counter to the dominant values and culture of the school. This included truancy, speaking in home language in the classroom, being late to lessons, 'chatting' in class and 'chatting back' – that is, challenging the teacher's authority. 'We mess around and get into trouble, we just have a laugh. Going places we shouldn't', was how one student (ZB) described it.

Policing sexuality and sexual reputation

Another important characteristic of this femininity was the policing of sexuality. A major consequence of forming all-girl groups was the rejection of male students in the school. All but one (TH) of the Gang girls consciously or purposely avoided boys, typically claiming, 'I hate boys' (PA). They showed a marked preference for female friendships, possibly to avoid the sexist abuse and name-calling which they applied to other girls who engaged in heterosexual relationships. They made judgements, as in Lees (1997), often employing sexist and abusive language to refer to female Asian students who associated with white students and especially with boys.

> There's a girl [****], in the third year. She acts like she's English. She goes out with boys like she hangs round with boys in school like she's got no

Asian friends and just every time hanging round with boys white boys. [People] swear, to her face and behind her back, 'slag', 'bitch'. Anything that comes into our minds, 'cause she's stupid going out with an English boy and she's Asian. (PA)

YA: Well she's got an English boyfriend and we always see her in [****] park, walking with him. We call her names.

FS: What sort of names?

YA: 'Slag', but she always calls us back then we get really angry.

Sexuality was an important mediating force in the working out of identities. The girls imply that to be a proper Asian girl one cannot associate with boys and associations with *white* boys represent the ultimate symbol of incorporation into the dominant white culture of the school. Although at one level there may exist a common experience as young, Asian and female, divisions exist between Asian girls that shape their experiences in school. The girls in this category experienced their sexuality in different ways to those in the other categories particularly the Rebels. Only one of the Gang girls was explicitly non-judgmental of Asian girls who were involved in heterosexual relationships.

Although the girls claimed not to have anything to do with boys, this was not entirely true. On one occasion, three girls were caught getting into a car driven by a young Asian man. The school made an assumption that the affair was sexual in nature but the girls protested at this assumption, insisting that the man was a relative of one of the girls. They also complained that their punishment – they were banned from leaving the school premises at lunch times for three months – was harsher than that applied to white girls who were routinely involved in similar activities.

Family

The Gang girls spoke positively about their families despite the restrictions they identified, such as not being allowed to go on to further education. Rather than resisting such restrictions or being overtly critical of their parents, a number of them appeared to have made a decision that school was a place to have fun. So they 'messed about' and attempted to discourage other Asian girls from working. They were very defensive about their families. TH defended her family when the school threatened to inform the Welfare services about her truancy, and HB spoke very positively about her family even as she justified her reason for not going to further education:

> My parents want the best for me because I'm the smallest in the family they want me to be happy, go out and enjoy life, not stuck in my books. Just kind of study but not take it to as far as university just to college and get a job soon after... I don't really want to go to university, I'll miss my family.

This could be interpreted as evidence against the cultural pathology discourse, since the young woman spoke highly of her family and did not appear unduly upset about the prospect of not attending university. There is also the possibility, however, that HB was providing a justification for the constraints that undoubtedly do exist for some Asian women. What is important, however, is the way she defined the situation she found herself in. She made a conscious decision to accept whatever constraints were imposed and avoid overt criticisms of her parents. Instead, like the other Gang girls, she prioritised racism as the main source of her oppression and thereby adopted strategies for defeating the boredom and irrelevance of studying, and this impacted negatively on her future chances.

Religion

Religion was an important means of self-definition for this group of girls but they interpreted it in terms of culture. All but one named religion as an important factor in their lives. Religion had different meanings and connotations for each girl. Even within the categories of Sikh or Muslim, there exist different interpretations and practices relating to the religion (Knott and Khoker, 1993; Mirza, 1989). Overall, religion was an important aspect in their lives which, in their view, differentiated them from other students in the school.

> I think it's important to know who you are and to respect the religion. Some people they don't respect or appreciate it. They want to live their own lives. That's okay but you should still remember your religion and you shouldn't hate your parents for giving you the religion. Some girls won't go to mosque or anything or when someone talks about religion they just start saying I'm not interested or it doesn't mean anything to me, but to me, it means a lot. I don't read Namaz or anything. I pray in my own way. (HB)

The Gang girls were the most likely to confuse religion with custom, as we can see:

> It affects me a lot... I always read the *Quoran* ... mixing with boys isn't in our religion, white boys I mean. (YA)

> Yeah like I'm a Muslim... I believe in Muslims. I think in life everyone has a chance to improve their life. If they lead a bad life they have a good life there [in heaven]. But I'm not religious in a way because I have a lot of fights, but I read the Quoran. Even if my mum doesn't say I still keep my head covered. (PA)

YA appears to believe that mixing with white boys is against her religion. This is based upon a misconception that all Muslims are Asian. PA believes that covering the head is an Islamic requirement. While this is a contentious issue, it is generally accepted that it is essential during prayer, and is subject to cultural variation on other occasions.

The girls can be seen to employ 'willing' and 'selective' conformity (Drury, 1991) in relation to religious ideology and practices. This suggests that they made conscious decisions about their lives and were involved in an active negotiation process, accepting some aspects of religion and neglecting or rejecting others.

> I've got to have religion, like my parents say and I'm still an Asian. I've got to obey the rules like getting an arranged marriage, reading *Namaz*, not going out with boys. Well, I obey some of them but I mix with boys, like as friends, but you have to listen to your parents sometimes. (TH)

Only one girl did not see religion as important:

> I don't know anything about my religion . . . I don't like learning. (AP)

AP's religious identity was secondary to her ethnic identity – that is she identified primarily as 'Asian'.

Future aspirations

All the Gang girls expected to be married in ten years time. None expected to make their own choice of partner or a love marriage. This reflected the gender relations within their home, but could also have resulted from their unwillingness to conform at school. From the responses of other girls in the study, it appeared that parents were prepared to delay marriages if their daughters intended to proceed with their studies. Consequently, the girls expected to marry after their studies had been completed. Only three of the Gang girls expected to combine marriage with a career.

None of this group gave the impression of living in fear of arranged marriages – as current media discourses imply, and none expressed a preference for a partner outside their ethnic or religious group. One young woman stated categorically that she was looking forward to her future marriage.

> FS: Where do you see yourself in ten years time?
>
> NP: I might be married. There's a lad, my chacha's (uncle's) son, I might get engaged to him [smiling]. He's quite handsome... don't tell anyone.

This challenges the dominant discourse of arranged marriages which suggests that many Asian girls are forced to marry strangers. Although a government commissioned report (cited in the *Guardian Unlimited* June 29th 2000; see also Samad and Eade, 2002) suggested that only a minority of Asian girls are now forced into such marriages, this discourse has again been appropriated to give added strength to Labour's calls for integration and community cohesion (CARF, 2002) as solutions to the social problems that provoked the inner city disturbances of 2001.

Although forced marriages are undoubtedly still practiced, what also needs to be acknowledged is the now common practice within many Asian communities for marriages to be result of negotiations, and often 'love marriages' are dressed up as arranged for the sake of the community. Such negotiation between parents and their daughters is described by HB:

> It depends, my parents, if I'm just messing around then they'd say something, but if I'm serious about somebody and I want to make it a serious relationship, instead of a one-off, then they won't mind because all of my brothers and sisters have had love marriages. Yeah, my two sisters have had love marriages. (HB)

The consequences of being a Gang girl

One of the major consequences of becoming one of the Gang girls was that the girls experienced negative relations with the staff of the school. This was largely because they appeared to challenge the dominant image of Asian girls as passive, quiet, shy. So the teachers did not quite know how to deal with them. Consequently, they spoke unfavourably of them, in terms such as 'troublemakers'. Some teachers openly confessed that they did not like the girls because of their involvement in these 'gangs'. The term itself has masculine connotations, associated as it is with boys, violence and laddishness and connects with wider discourses on Asian masculinity that position them as hot-headed and volatile. The fact that the girls were subjected to physical abuse that provoked them to respond in a physical way further reinforces this masculinisation of her femininity.

Immediate gratification was another major Gang characteristic. The girls were in the bottom sets and teachers viewed them as academically incapable. They claimed to receive little or no encouragement from the school and staff and because they felt misunderstood, they resorted to strategies to defeat boredom, some of which involved breaking school rules, truanting and being late for lessons.

> I don't trust teachers... I was in a fight once and she [teacher] said I was shit-stirring, causing trouble, and that I caused the fight and everything. She's not nice to me. She treats the whites properly... I just swear at her... I was all right until I started to get into trouble last year. (NN)
>
> Teachers, some of them are all right. We really mess around a lot, just talk. When we get bored we just start talking. (ZB)

They also claimed to have been treated more harshly by the school when they broke rules. This suggests that common-sense assumptions about Asian girls as shy and timid may prejudice teachers in their interactions with those who challenge these assumptions.

> I think they're racist to tell you the truth. They know the Asians' parents are stricter so they get on to 'em. Say, an Asian person truanted and a white person truanted as well. Well, they'd just tell the white person off, or send a letter. But they'd ring the Asian parents. (TH)

Although this statement is expressed hypothetically, it in fact refers to the incident alluded to earlier, when the school employed its Asian teachers to inform TH's parents of her poor attendance at school. As a result of this knowledge her parents withdrew their permission for her to continue her studies beyond compulsory schooling. Another young woman was suspended for fighting during a critical exam period and consequently missed a number of important exams. This illustrates the serious consequences of stereotyping and pathologising young Asian women.

> About two weeks ago the girl didn't get into much trouble. They let her
> get away with it. she said she wasn't really aiming at me but it does hurt
> inside when she says, 'a gang of Pakis'. So I went to get her but I didn't hit
> her and she told the teacher, and I got into trouble. (NB)

This young woman clearly felt that she had been treated harshly by the school. In her view, the school had allowed racist behaviour to go unchecked precisely because she was perceived to be part of an Asian girl gang. Both incidents cited above reflect the ways in which common-sense ideas informing the routine practices of teaching are shaped by racial ideologies that can have material effects on the students (Parmar, 1988). The girls who refused to conform to the stereotype of quietness and meekness were frequently labelled by teachers as a trouble-makers. Asian girls who do not conform to the shy, timid and quiet stereotype can be treated more harshly than other girls when they break school rules. Punishments were more severe precisely because these girls challenged what was expected and acceptable behaviour. By not conforming to the stereotypes, such girls may be labelled as threatening, particularly when in all-Asian girl groups, and subjected to further racial abuse and physical attack.

In their rejection of schooling, however, the young women played an active part in the reproduction of the conditions of their oppression. Not only did staff speak about them unfavourably but white students were also critical of them because they appeared to be exclusive, due to their using home language as a weapon and opting for all female friendships. The term 'gang of Pakis' was often employed by other students to describe them. The criticism was also levelled at them from other Asian girls in the school, most notably the Rebels.

The Gang girls were believed actively to discourage other Asian girls from studying because they themselves had no support from their parents for studying further. Having abandoned any desire to succeed themselves, they tried, girls such as AH thought, to abort the efforts of those who were academically successful: 'These Pakistani girls mainly, they discourage you. So, my dad tells me not to mix with them that much'.

As their families received no positive reports from the school and because there was rarely any contact between the school and these families, it was foregone conclusion that the Gang girls would not pursue further studies. Accordingly, they had extremely low expectations of academic success and further study:

> AP: I can't read or write. I just don't be bothered. It's boring English. I just don't like the teacher he's always picking on us, all the Asian girls.
>
> FS: Can you comment on your progress?
>
> AP: I don't know, I hardly come into school. I'm in the lower sets.
>
> FS: Do you have any career plans?
>
> AP: I'm not interested. I don't want to do anything. I just like coming to meet my friends.

By challenging the dominant stereotypes of passive and timid Asian girls, the girls played a crucial role in the creation of an Asian femininity from which others (white students and other students who appeared to them as allying with white students) were excluded. Educational mobility did not play a part in the struggle to assert the hegemony of this femininity. In identifying the main cause of their oppression as racism, they appeared to accept and provide justification for the likelihood by their families of their exclusion from further education and careers. It was their definition and acceptance of the inevitability of this situation that shaped their behaviour. Consequently, they viewed school as a place to have fun and defeat boredom. They also made attempts to convince other girls of the inevitability of their future roles as wives and mothers. Inherent in this view was a fatalism that owed as much to their class locations in England as to their cultural backgrounds: they believed that change was not possible. Thus rather than being passive, the girls played an active part in the reproduction of the conditions of their oppression.

5

The Survivors

The girls in the category I call the 'Survivors', could be identified as pro-education but not as anti-schooling, because they did not see schooling as irrelevant or boring. In this respect, they differ from the Black Sisters in Mac an Ghaill's (1988) study, who responded to their schooling in terms of a strategy which was 'anti school but pro education' that is, they rejected the racist curriculum but greatly valued the acquisition of academic qualifications.

In comparison to the Gang girls, this group of twelve girls defined their experiences of schooling in positive terms. They conformed in many ways to the concept of the 'ideal pupil' by working hard to achieve success and by avoiding confrontation and other behaviour that ran counter to school rules. In this sense they were less visible than the Gang girls because they did not present a cause for concern. Teachers referred to them as 'nice girls' and as 'good workers'. This was mainly because they conformed to the dominant stereotype of Asian girls as shy and timid, passive and quiet. Their accounts, however, revealed that rather than being timid or passive, the girls were actively engaged in a strategy for self-advancement through education – that is, they actively avoided trouble and worked hard in the hope that they might change their present circumstances. So their apparent conformity was part of a broader coping strategy that also involved a series of negotiations in their home lives.

Although the girls spoke mainly in positive terms about their experiences of schooling, this did not mean that they denied the existence of racism and or sexism. They showed awareness of such issues but chose to adopt a different method for dealing with this than the Gang girls did. Rather than overtly expressing opposition they chose to ignore manifestations of sexism and racism:

PM: The teachers are trying to get the Christians and Muslims together by saying its part of their religion but it doesn't matter whether its part of their religion or not. People will still be racist even when you get black Christians, it's still racist. It doesn't matter if it's part of your religion, people just see you as your colour.

FS: Do you feel people see you as your colour?

PM: No not really. I'm a loud talkative person. My friends don't see me as my colour. I don't talk about Asian rights and that, they see me as normal.

FS: Who talks about Asian rights?

PM: No one, because they might think we're talking about Asian rights, racism [– but it] will always be there in twenty years time but we have to deal with that.

FS: How?

PM: That's another thing. All I do is ignore it because if you show it hurts you then they keep prodding at you like it's in a sense bullying. I just ignore them or say something sarcastic back. I wouldn't say anything racist because then you're as bad as them. I'm not racist. Anyhow let people be what they like, let people have their own opinions.

PM's remarks are particularly revealing of the ways in which racism impacts on the girls' schooling. Following a number of violent incidents in the school, the headteacher called a special assembly to bring the issue out in the open, trying to find common ground through the theme of religion. PM here has internalised the view that talking about racism equates to pressing for 'Asian rights', which implies a political cause rather than a response to provocation. Her account also reveals that the girls who talk about racism or attempt to deal directly with the issue are branded as 'not normal'. PM chooses to deal with the issue of racism by ignoring it. Her justification is that fighting back produces further rebuttal in the form of racist bullying, so the only option is to ignore it.

This was a common approach for the girls in this category. Their responses to racism involved at most a verbal rebuke. It was this strategy of being seen as not fighting back that helped them to be regarded by teachers as ideal or model pupils and thus have positive relations with them.

Teachers

The Gang girls spoke in strongly negative terms about their interactions with teachers but the Survivors viewed teachers more positively. The majority found teachers to be 'helpful or encouraging'. Only one said teachers were racist. Another girl went as far as to suggest that Asian girls sometimes manipulated racism for their own ends:

> They're not really racist, but it's that many Asian girls start chatting and if they're told off by the teacher, they think it's racist. (SL)

So although Asian girls are subject to common experiences of discrimination, based on their economic and geographical location in England, they define their experiences of schooling in different ways. The teachers also differentiated, viewing the Survivors as hardworking and quiet and not as trouble-makers, so there was little antagonism here. This also suggested why the girls did not particularly want to see more Asian teachers in the school.

Asian teachers

The Gang girls expressed a desire to see more Asian teachers in the school because they felt they would be more sympathetic to their concerns, on grounds of an (assumed) shared sense of ethnic identity. For the Survivors, however, educational performance was the key factor in shaping their definition of schooling and only four of these girls favoured more Asian staff. And their reason was not because they felt personally misunderstood by mainstream teachers, as the Gang girls did but because they felt other Asian students might benefit.

> I think there should be more Asian teachers teaching other subjects as well [as Urdu] – children are shy – I was shy with the English teachers before but now it's much easier for me. (SL)

> Only if they can teach properly. (SP)

What these comments reveal is that the key concern for these girls was not ethnic background but the teacher's ability to deal with Asian students who are intimidated by white mainstream teachers and particularly to teach competently. One reason the girls did not turn to Asian teachers for support was that they experienced relatively positive relations with mainstream (white) teachers who did not regard them a trouble-makers because of their reputation for being quiet and shy. Another factor that helped to build their reputations as ideal pupils was these girls' involvement in friendship groups that crossed ethnic boundaries.

Friendship patterns

Friendship patterns were one of the clearest areas in which a conscious strategy of survival was being operated. All the girls indicated that they purposely chose friends from different ethnic backgrounds to their own. ZK confessed that aside from the fact that few Asian girls were in her form, she chose to mix with white girls specifically in order to avoid racist name-calling.

> FS: Why do you have English friends instead of just Asians?
>
> ZK: Because it's not nice being called names especially in front of a whole class ... a lot of them stick up for me. They say 'if anyone calls you anything you tell me ... you're protected'... I'm protected by them. It's nothing I do, I just mix with them. I just know how to talk to 'em. Since I was little, I've always mixed with English girls. There's girls here who were in my primary school class but I've drifted away from them. I say 'hi' to them but they talk about Pakistani things like marriages ... and I don't know about these things. I think as I said I choose to stick with white girls to have less trouble. But I also stick with them, because they're the only ones in my classes.

Because girls like ZK did not associate closely with Asian girl gangs they were vulnerable to abuse. They were also vulnerable because there were fewer Asian students in the higher sets. To avoid racist name-calling, the girls apparently needed to build alliances with white school mates who might protect them, thus reinforcing their passive image. If they do not mix, they are seen as refusing to integrate. As I argued earlier, this resonates with wider national political discourses on race and integration such as espoused by the current Home Secretary in relation to asylum seekers.

The girls deliberately tried to associate with all ethnic groups in the school. Avoidance of particular individuals or groups was based not upon ethnicity but upon a wider set of criteria, which related to the breaking of school rules. They avoided, for instance, 'smokers' and 'people with bad reputations'. They made a deliberate effort not be judgmental of other students, as can be seen in the following response, where PM defends a white girl who has been labelled both 'slag' and 'racist'.

...Even English people say she's a tart and everything. All that swearing and they kind of say bad things about her but I've got to know her, I think she's nice. I'm not really bothered what she does. What she does is her own time. It's nothing to do with her personality. I don't mind her. Like I do have one friend, not really a friend, who's very racist. I did talk to her once ... she seemed all right like she is tough and cocky and everything but she only fights people who say things to her. She doesn't just pick on anybody. She seemed all right ... When you hear about somebody and you think and you don't even know 'em they group you in saying 'she's bad' or after hearing about a couple of fights, Asian people say racist things. (PM)

This comment highlights the difference in experiences among the Asian girls in the school. While the Gang girls viewed white students as 'the enemy', the Survivors were prepared to defend them. So their experiences of and approaches to schooling differed, as the Survivors prioritised educational advancement and sought to avoid trouble at all costs.

Dress

For the Gang girls traditional dress was an important and visible symbol of their defiance of what they perceived as the dominant white culture of the school. The Survivors, however, wore clothing appropriate to context – that is, they did not use dress to actively resist either parent culture or western culture. Only two of the girls wore western clothes on all occasions:

I don't feel comfortable in salwar-kameez and that so I just wear trousers at home. I hate silk. (AH)

I just wear jeans and t-shirt. I feel more comfortable. (PP)

Both girls had parental permission to dress in western style so were not using western dress as a means to resist parental regimes. This again illustrates how the girls' households differed in their gender patterns.

In compliance with the wishes of their parents, two of the girls wore salwar-kameez. Although they did not object on principle, they indicated that they would have preferred to have some choice in the matter. But this did not lead them to rebel and wear western clothing in defiance of their parent's wishes. Instead, we see unwilling conformity, where parents' wishes were reluctantly obeyed (Drury, 1991).

SS: My dad is strict. If I had the choice I would wear English [clothes]

FS: Why is that?

SS: To avoid being called 'Paki'.

So wearing traditional Asian clothing, like mixing only with the Asian girls, evidently provokes racist name-calling. Apparently girls who wear western clothing are more readily considered acceptable. This exerts pressure on Asian girls to conform but, as we saw in the last chapter, the Gang girls were prepared to face the consequences of defending their traditional clothing. Some of the Survivors also claimed that they were neither embarrassed nor ashamed to wear traditional Asian clothing and usually wore it at home for traditional functions but wore western clothing in public. They therefore displayed apparent conformity in appropriate contexts, which was all part of their overall survival strategy. Had they actively resisted by wearing western clothing in open defiance of their parents, they would have risked losing their parents' trust and support, which they needed in order to pursue their long-term goals of academic success. But if they wore traditional clothes, even as part of the uniform of the school, they might be seen as refusing to integrate and suffer the consequences the Gang girls experience in their relations with staff and students in the school. Their survival strategies involved wearing the most acceptable clothes for each setting. The girls were not 'confused' or 'caught between two cultures'; they had made conscious decisions to wear context-appropriate clothing in order maintain the respect of their parents and to succeed at school.

> I think it's respectable to wear it [traditional dress] at home, because my mum lets me wear English clothes. I should keep that outside, inside I should stay Muslim. (ZK)

When she wore western clothes, ZK did not overstep the mark by wearing skirts, but struck instead a careful balance between the wishes of her mother and the demands of western fashions. Western dress was therefore limited to trousers.

Language

The Survivors did not perceive the school's official language as a major instrument of their own deculturalisation (Mac an Ghaill, 1988). Although none of them used language as a mechanism of white exclusion, this did not mean that they were ashamed or embarrassed to use their home language when required, for example when helping other students with language difficulties. Rather than using it as a weapon or ex-clusionary mechanism, the girls spoke of the offence its use might cause. They were wary of using it 'unnecessarily' lest it offend people who couldn't understand. As ZK argued, 'I don't use it too often be-cause English girls take offence'.

Academic progress and career aspirations

Based on his research findings in a study in Southall, Bains (1988) argues that a double standard operated in Punjabi households. Boys were expected to go out to work, to support the family and raise its status.

> Consequently, their view of schooling is highly instrumental – it is just a means of earning credentials to be cashed into good jobs. Girls, in contrast, are still largely viewed in economically inactive terms. Their primary role is to maintain the household, first while with their parents and later for their husband. Girls consequently tend to view staying on at school as a means of holding some of these pressures in abeyance. Exam successes become symbols of independence, a means of establishing an existence outside the all-consuming home life. Girls are much more acutely aware of the double standards operated both within their own families and within the school. But equally their dependence on academic success as a way of sustaining some critical instance from Punjabi family ideology makes them fearful of 'burning their boats' by challenging the school regime as well. (Bains, 1988:232)

The girls in the Survivor category appeared unwilling to burn their boats by challenging either family or school. Compared with the Gang girls, the Survivors had a much clearer idea of where they wished to be in ten years time and adopted a careful strategy to win support from both school and family to get there. ZK, who wished to pursue a career in law, managed to win the firm support of her mother by not actively resisting the wishes of her parents. In return for this support, she com-mented, 'I'll do anything for my mum. First it's my mum, then religion and the family'

The pursuit of academic and career success was viewed by the Sur-vivors as one way of expanding horizons for themselves, for their families and ultimately for Asian communities:

PM: I don't want [to be a] drop-out. Most people think Asian people are dumb, stupid, don't know anything, they don't try at school. Well, quite a number of Asians do really well. They get higher than a lot of other races in school. I mean in class. So I want to do well ... I want to do some profession that a lot of males do. I feel like I want to prove something, something a male can do. I wouldn't mind doing engineering or something maybe only white people do ... do something that's not typical because most people round our area, the job they've got is either housewife or craft like sewing ... most Asian women tend to be a secretary. I don't want to be a secretary. That's the last thing I want to do. Males are usually waiters. I don't want to be a waiter. I just want to do something that I can travel a lot – like art and design – and I get good marks so I don't mind doing it.

FS: Why do you feel you want to do something that Asians don't usually do?

PM: I don't know. I just want to do something different. It could be like saying open a door for Asians – it sounds a bit stupid – but I'd like to do something different because I want to change it. All Asians do something typical. I want to do something different than a second class job, a typical job. I don't want something very feminist, just different because I'm an all round type of person.

PM is showing an experiential understanding of the ways Asians and Asian women in particular are marginalised to particular kinds of work. She therefore sets out her aspirations to challenge this situation, albeit at an individual level, by striving for educational qualifications. What needs to be noted here however, is that although she might succeed educationally in terms of gaining academic qualifications, other barriers still exist in the work-place (cf Mirza, 1992) who found that despite doing well in terms of gaining qualifications, African-Caribbean women were discriminated against in the labour market on grounds of ethnicity and gender. Current employment statistics also reveal that only 24.7% of Pakistani and Bangladeshi women are economically active compared with 70.9% of white women, 57.6% of black (African Caribbean women and 60.1% of Indian women (Office for National Statistics, 2002).

Family
Bains (1988) also argues that although Asian students experience a variety of home backgrounds, parents originating from villages in

Punjab (like those of many of the girls in this study) tend to be less well educated, do less well economically in the UK and to be more traditionalist in their orientation, whereas those with higher incomes tend to be 'more willing to trade off their culture for material benefits which they think acceptance of their children by white society will bring to the whole family. Consequently these parents tend to give their children more room to manoeuvre at home' (1988: 233).

Following Gramsci, one of my arguments is that these girls take an active role in making room for themselves through their various survival strategies and coping mechanisms. This is true not only in the context of the family but also in the school, where Asian girls are faced with the dominant culture's stereotypical assumptions of them as passive, timid and as the victims of backward and barbaric cultural practices. PM's father, who was a cotton doubler, positively encouraged her to proceed with education because it offered her opportunities and a 'way out' of the situations he had faced as a manual labourer. His experience of working in northern mills is a common one for Asian men of his generation who arrived to support the post-war effort in England but found themselves working difficult and unsocial shifts. Many were made redundant as factories closed, and had little hope of finding alternative employment. The local economic context as it was mediated through her father's experiences played a crucial role in shaping PM's survival strategy.

Other Survivors were also encouraged by their families and spoke positively about their families and, contrary to the dominant discourse of Asian femininity, they did not view the worlds of home and school as fundamentally opposed. Although they did not automatically receive support from either their families or the school, support was won through a carefully worked out strategy, which involved a series of negotiations. SL asserted that she would not take any course of action that would be offensive to her parents because of the support and encouragement they gave her.

> My parents are worried about us because we are six daughters and they don't want us to get up to anything but they're not always behind our backs or spying on us like most parents do. They trust us but they expect us to keep that trust. (SL)

She went on to defend parents' strategies regarding arranged marriages, by reversing the charge. It was the parents, in her view, who were 'forced' into such decisions by their daughters' actions.

> Parents are right. People who have arranged marriages, it's because of what they've been up to in school. They've forced their parents to do something. We had some neighbours ... the daughter was always going out with boys and always causing hassles for her parents but she married to someone she loved. (SL)

The focus is once more on not rocking the boat. You must be respectful to your family otherwise you give them no choice but to act in this way – that is, send you back home to Pakistan. The trust the girls won was carefully secured and they did not want to endanger it by engaging in activities that ran counter to school rules, so avoided any situation that put their parents' respect at risk, including how they interacted with boys.

Opposite sex

None of the girls were prepared to admit to being involved in romantic relationships themselves. Some did confess to mixing with boys but not in the context of a romantic relationship.

> I talk to them in class. My dad doesn't stop me, but if I go up to them outside of class it's different. (AH)

Though they did not confess to engaging in heterosexual relationships they were significantly non-judgmental of the other girls who did involve themselves. This was in marked contrast with the Gang girls.

> JB: I don't care if they want to go out with them they can.
>
> FS: And for yourself?
>
> JB: No I don't think it's right.

Only one girl expressed disappointment with the girls who were romantically involved with boys. However it was not just the incorporation this symbolised into the dominant white culture of the school, but rather the betrayal of her parents' trust, which for her was of paramount importance.

> There's a lot of Asian girls who go out with boys and I hate them y'know. Because I know it's against our religion. If that's what they want to do they

> can but the thing I don't like about them is they're two-faced. Because they can tell me that they go out with boys and people but I already know but I mean my mum trusts me and she knows I'll never do that. *I know I'll never get that trust back off her.* My mum trusts me and lets me go out on my own. (ZK, my emphasis)

It was the experience of family and in particular her relationship with her mother that differentiated ZK's approach to schooling from that of other Asian girls that she describes as 'two-faced'. Like SL, the trust and support of her mother for her education had been carefully secured and becoming involved in a heterosexual relationship could potentially destroy that trust. ZK also expressed a dislike of Asian boys, whom she saw as having double standards.

> I hate them! I don't talk to them at all because all the Asian boys in this school go out with girls and stuff and when they look at me, they look at me in a really dirty way. Just because you wear English clothes, they think y'know, the boys in this school they all stare at you and I hate it but I don't talk to them. I talk to English boys. They don't stare at you. (ZK)

An important theme highlighted by this response is that of sexual labelling – this time by the boys. As Hargreaves (1990) also found, Asian boys sometimes operate double standards. Asian girls and young women attending bhangras were regarded as 'loose', compared with 'respectful' Asian girls who obeyed their parents and stayed at home, but the boys also expected to be able to interact with the girls who did attend. So the girls were considered 'fair game' and fights broke out among the boys and men who tried to protect their own sisters and girl-friends from preying men.

Name-calling

We noted in the section on friendship that identification with the Asian girl groups in the school had consequences both in terms of negative relations with teachers and students and potential racial abuse. It was this awareness that motivated the Survivors' association with mainly white students so as to avoid being subjected to racist name-calling. Though such strategies protected them from name-calling in the school, they did not guarantee protection outside.

> SS: It doesn't happen in school that much but outside school it does. 'Paki', 'Get out of this country', 'It's not your country'.

FS: How do you feel?

SS: I'm not a Muslim. They don't know that, but I feel bad. Just because its not our country doesn't mean we can't stay in it. I mean English people go to India don't they?

FS: When they say Paki, what do you think they mean?

SS: They think I'm Muslim then.

Clearly SS associates being a 'Paki' with being a Muslim. This highlights the contested nature of the racist term of abuse, particularly in the wake of the Rushdie affair and the Gulf War in the early 1990s and the recent representations of Muslims as terrorists. All these are key events in the racialisation of religion (Modood, 1992, Miles, 1993, Solomos and Back, 1994) that appears to be internalised here. This example also illustrates how Asian girls are both positioned and position themselves in relation to such discourses (Mani and Frankenburg, 1993). Defining herself as an Indian Sikh and therefore non-Muslim, SS is able to dissociate herself from a label that has its roots in the period of racialised immigration politics in the 1950s and 60s (Solomos, 1992). However, the label continues to be applied to perceived members of the Asian community. As I have argued, some Sikhs and Hindus may currently position themselves as outside the global discourse of terrorism that is applied to Muslim communities but are often positioned within it because of their visible similarity to Muslims. This can lead to severe consequences, as in the case of the Sikh man murdered in America in 'revenge' for the terrorist attack on September 11, 2001. In England two Sikh councillors were 'mistaken' for Muslims and also attacked (CRE, 2002).

We have seen that racism and racist name-calling are part of daily experience for many Asian students (Troyna, 1987, Wright, 1992). The girls in this category did not escape racist name-calling despite their survival strategies of mixing across ethnic groups. Only three claimed to have never been called a racist name. The six girls who confessed to having been racially abused generally tried to ignore such abuse. SP for example said, 'I feel bad but there's nothing you can do about it'. One girl chose to form friendships with English girls to avoid being called names, while another claimed that by ignoring racist insults, she protected herself from receiving further abuse. These girls were less likely to actively resist name-calling and although they retorted verbally on occasion, for example, 'I'm proud to be a Paki!' (AH), they did not involve themselves in fighting lest they be labelled trouble-makers like the Gang girls.

Religion

Religion was important to the social identity of the girls and all but one identified religion as important. The one who did not came from a family who was not religious either, so reflecting established non conformity (Drury, 1991).

> Not much. I don't find religion important or anything. They say you should like read the *Quoran* every day. My dad's not religious. He just likes us to behave ourselves and not to be silly at school. (SP)

The survival techniques employed by the girls had a bearing on their views on religion. Rather than blindly accepting religious teachings from parents or religious teachers, the girls made active decisions about which aspects of religion they would accept or reject and in which contexts. They engaged in a process in which new religious identities were being created through a reinterpretation of existing religious values in new (English) contexts. Most of the girls showed an ability to distinguish between religion and social practice. A young Hindu woman, for example, told me:

> We're supposed to be vegetarian ... then it comes down to caste, that's nothing to do with religion, it's with society and everything. One thing, because we're religious they say don't do this, don't do that because of your religion and then they're not even vegetarian and that's the main thing. The priest he's a right idiot, he doesn't even know what to do. (PM)

Talking about her own personal approach to religion, PM maintained that she did not accept the prevailing religious values blindly but was capable of distinguishing between religion and custom.

> Sometimes you do need to know your religion to find yourself in a sense. It is important to me but I wouldn't let it ruin my life. ...It may not make you do certain things but you just do it.. You've gotten so used to doing certain things like most of it it's superstition. Like don't cut your nails on a certain day or don't have cabbage at night because you become poor. [LAUGHS] That IS thick! If I lived in Bradford I'd probably have more understanding of my religion. (PM)

PM's remark indicates the significance of regional location in shaping the experiences of Asian girls and consequently their responses. Because she lives in a predominantly Muslim neighbourhood PM has different experiences to girls in Hindu communities – which would offer a stronger support network.

For Muslim girls, wearing of *hijab,* reading the *Quoran* and not going out with boys were identified as important, while for Sikh girls going to the Sikh temple, not going out with boys and not cutting their hair were prioritised. Thus, similarities and differences were found in their experiences of religion and this can be seen in the following two comments. The first is from a Muslim and the second from a Sikh girl:

> Sometimes I hate being a Muslim. I think it's too much hassle like keeping a scarf with you which I don't really but I've been told to do. My mum's pressured me into doing things .. It [religion] is important and it isn't. She doesn't say 'wear it' she says keep it round your neck but sometimes I do and sometimes I don't. (SL)

> [Religion is important] in many ways like for example not to cut your hair before marriage, not to go off with boys, read the holy book. I believe in God and go to the Gurdwara [Sikh temple]. (SS)

Future aspirations

Only one of the girls did not expect to combine marriage with a successful career. The Survivors did not view marriage as something to be forced into. They saw themselves playing an active part in choice of marriage partner, in a future negotiation. None of the girls expected to marry outside their religious or ethnic group and all were positive about their future prospects:

> I'd probably be married. I don't know really. If I carry on I don't think I'll be married ... [Marriage] will be my parents' choice but they'll ask me first. I'll stick to the family like I won't do anything against them. (SL)

> [I'll be] married [with] ten kids! [LAUGHS] .. I want someone who would let me have my freedom. Y'know let me get a job and support me as well, I'd like to support him in a sense. He would have to be Hindu, in our religion obviously it would be a scandal otherwise. (PM)

> I want to marry someone who's born in England. I think he'd have to be Asian because in my religion you're not meant to get married to white people unless he's a Muslim. So if he became a Muslim, even if he's white,

it could be all right by me. As long as he has some faith in Islam, I don't mind. ...It's up to my parents really. If he's an Islamic English then, not totally English. It's a *Kafer* (sin) you know what I'm talking about. (AH)

The girls showed conformity with their parents' religious practices. None was against religion but they showed they had made some reinterpretation of traditional religious values in relation to their local contexts.

The consequences of being a Survivor

Those who adopted the survival strategy appeared to conform to the stereotype of quiet, timid, shy and obedient Asian girls rather than challenging it. This made them more acceptable to the white students and teachers in the school.

A major consequence of adopting this strategy was deferred gratification. Academic success was their key motivation and it spurred them on in school. So they did not break the rules by defying the teacher's authority or truanting.

Their dissociation from Asian girl groups to avoid being labelled accordingly and their conformity to stereotypes contributed to the positive perception of the Survivors generally held by teachers and students. These girls' survival strategies have the potential to facilitate their access into higher and further education. Their individualistic hardworking strategies could win the support and approval of teachers and parents for them to pursue further education. However discrimination in the labour market must not be underestimated (Mirza, 1992), as the figures in chapter one suggest. As a consequence of their actions, for example, their determined dissociation from Asian girl gangs and their willingness to mix with different groups in the school, they were viewed as 'more willing to integrate' by the white students in the school and so more positively.

However, the Gang girls and the Asian boys viewed them as 'stuck up', because they were seen to mix with white students.

These girls' survival strategies began at home, and they won support from their parents by their strategy of deferred gratification. They did not rebel against their parents' views. Their careful strategy was designed to ensure maximum support from parents.

Within the context of the school, the girls appeared to be conforming to the predominant stereotypes of passive, timid Asian girls, but they were playing for potentially positive future consequences. By deferring gratification they not only challenged the dominant view in wider society that Asian girls were not allowed to proceed into higher education but they were also contributing to making higher education more accessible for other Asian girls. However, these determinedly-followed strategies might ultimately not withstand the impact of racial and gender discrimination in the labour market.

6

The Rebels

The girls in this category, whom I've called the 'Rebels', prioritised uneven gender relations in their experience of family and community. This, above all, influenced their approaches to schooling. Although they sometimes expressed criticism of parental cultures, they also identified positive experiences in their family and community life. In school their adoption of western modes of dress and their active dissociation from Asian girl groups were influential in increasing their popularity with teachers and students, as compared with the Asian girl groups. They were not perceived to be maintaining an exclusionary and separate Asian identity based on a common experience of racism. Although they encountered racism they did not see it as the main cause of their oppression. Instead, their prioritisation of uneven gender relations within their communities led some of them to regard their parents' views as 'backward'. Such views indicated their internalisation of racist ideologies and this was further evidenced by their negative descriptions of other Asian pupils. Some of the girls routinely employed the racist term of abuse, 'Paki' to describe other Asians, as RE does below.

In their everyday experiences of school, the Rebels employed a survival strategy which prioritised academic success. They spoke more positively than other Asian girls in their schools about their schooling. RE for example, talks of being more comfortable at school than at home:

> I like school, the teachers are good. It's just I don't like holidays. I'd rather stay at school than go home. [my mother is] always 'bragging' ... she starts reading *Namaz* [prayers]. She never does though and she thinks she's dead holy and everything ordering all those stupid cassettes. And all these Pakis come telling her how we are.

RE adopts the dominant discourse of Asian femininity, positioning herself as a victim of familial and cultural practices. The 'Pakis' she refers to are community members (friends and extended family) who apparently police and regulate their behaviour by informing parents of the (mis)conduct of their children. She equates the school with positive experiences that she does not experience in the home, which is characterised as restrictive. Although this approach influenced her attitudes towards other Asian girls in the school, she did not deny that racist name-calling was common there.

Teachers

The Rebels maintained positive relations with mainstream teachers and most of the group felt that their teachers were 'good' or 'encouraging '. Only two spoke about teachers in connection with racism:

> Sometimes, the teachers can be biased against coloureds. (SB)

> The teachers are okay. Some of them are a bit racist but we put up with them. (SJ)

The latter response in particular is typical of the confidence exhibited by this group. SJ is able to seize power from teachers by reversing the usual case and suggesting that it is they, the students, who put up with teachers who might be racist. Racism was therefore categorised as more of an annoyance than a source of oppression.

Asian teachers

The Rebels were also critical of Asian teachers. They expressed little desire to see more in the school. They perceived school space as positive and sought positive relations with mainstream white staff. None of the Rebels felt any need for Asian teachers and two of them challenged their competence:

> SJ: No there's only the ones that teach Urdu that's it.

> FS: Would you like to see more [Asian teachers]?

> SJ: Well I wouldn't mind. Some of them though they teach a bit funny. We had some that were starting out as teachers and they didn't know what they were on about ... [people] didn't like them at all. They didn't know how to teach. They just wanted you to get on with it and they just stood there. So we really messed up while they were around.

RH: Two or three that's it. [They teach] Urdu ... I wish they'd teach something else but normally when an Asian teacher teaches the kids don't listen to them.

FS: Why?

RH: Because the Asian teachers they don't take any notice.

Asian teachers are characterised here by their lack of ability to teach or control classes and no blame is allocated to the pupils for their unruly behaviour. The implication that they are not up to the job reinforces the marginal status of Asian teachers in the school and the fact that the girls did not see them as positive role-models.

Dress

An important characteristic of being a Rebel was their expressed preference for 'English' or western clothing. Three girls wore western dress with the permission of parents, thereby exhibiting established non-conformity. Two Muslim girls appeared to be resisting their culture by revealing their bare legs, but both had their parents' approval and in this respect had more in common with two of the Sikh girls in the sample than with other Muslim girls. One of the Muslim girls mentioned above wore skirts to school and 'skirts and leggings' at home. She said that her father, who apparently believed that traditional clothes are more revealing of the body, actively encouraged this:

FH: I only dress traditional at weddings. My dad prefers us in English clothes because Asian clothes show your figure more and men look more and it's better when you've got English clothes on. You can tell you're young. When you're married you will have to wear Asian clothes anyway.

FS: Do you get fewer looks in English clothes?

FH: No [Laughs]

Just as the Gang girls provided justifications for their appropriation of traditional dress, so FH attempts to provide a justification for her western mode of dress – although she does not share father's view that western clothes are less revealing. An Indian Sikh girl offered this justification for adopting western dress:

[My father] says you're over here, so you might as well behave as though you're here and not get left out. Part of what causes the trouble is the way people dress and how they stick to what they've come from, like if they come from India or Pakistan. They stick to there ... They think they can do as they please. That's a really big part of racial discrimination, the way they are themselves. (NS)

The message that appears to have been internalised by this girl, whose family lived in an area inhabited by diverse groups and away from concentrations of Asian communities, is that to avoid racial discrimination Asians must abandon any inclination towards Indian or Pakistani cultures from 'back home'. She views such behaviour as symbolic of a refusal to integrate into British society, an assumption that guided her strategy. The Rebels strongly dissociated from the Gang girls, whose behaviour they perceived as a rejection of British identity. This resonates strongly with the Home Secretary's pronouncements in 2002 on race and integration. Although Mr Blunkett was speaking mainly about language issues with regard to asylum seekers, the underlying assumption is that racial discrimination can be avoided if attempts are made to integrate (CARF, 2002). The pressure on Asian girls to conform places a burden especially on those who wear *hijab*.

The Rebels' experiences also illustrate the powerful role that schooling plays in policing the boundaries of acceptability. Three of the Rebels felt 'awkward' or 'uncomfortable' in Asian clothes, particularly in front of their white peers. One girl was afraid her white friends 'might laugh' (AA) and another, KP, signalled her ambivalence about the issue thus:

KP: I've always worn [salwar-kameez]. Sometimes, when I'm going out I wear jeans and trousers, sometimes salwar-kameez [when I'm going] out. At school, I wear trousers. My mum likes to say [that] my dad doesn't like it. My dad never says anything. I think it's my mum. I feel awkward wearing trousers at home unless I'm wearing a really baggy T shirt over them or something.

FS: Why is that?

KP: I don't know – It's because of what my mum says, 'your dad doesn't like it'. He doesn't say anything, but I know I can just sense it so as soon as I get home I get changed. It's salwar-kameez at home. ... I prefer trousers. ... I don't really mind ... To go out I'd wear trousers, it's more comfortable and they look better. Sometimes I feel weird wearing salwar-kameez in front of my English friends.

FS: Why is that?

KP: I don't know ... because I think it shows that I'm under the thumb of my parents, because I'm not allowed out in the way they are and so when I'm wearing these clothes, it's showing them that my mum and dad still control me a lot. Not as much as they might want to but they still do. I feel uncomfortable sometimes but I'm wearing these clothes because I like them. So it doesn't matter.

Her response suggests an internalisation of her father's disapproval and this limits her behaviour and prevents her from resisting actively. Her fear that friends might think she is being controlled by her parents is another example of the ways the cultural pathology framework enters into the site of peer relations. Traditional clothing is read here as sign of being over-controlled by parents. KP's comments also reflect the importance of local and regional influences on fashion and the fact that she lives in a city associated with fashion cannot be discounted.

Language
Like dress, language was another important site for contesting the boundaries of acceptability and the Rebels expressed strong feelings about the issue of home languages being spoken in school.

None of the girls used language as a weapon or a mechanism for white exclusion (Mac an Ghaill, 1988). This is related to the fact that over half the Rebels had exclusively white friendships and the others mixed. So using home language in the school was considered impolite. There was no antagonism between themselves and white students and teachers, who, for the majority, were preferred as friends and teachers. Another characteristic of the Rebels was their acceptance that Asians should 'integrate into' western societies.

...you sound daft [speaking Punjabi in school] because it's an English school, you should speak English. I feel comfortable in English. These Pakistani girls speaking Punjabi, they don't speak at a normal level. They shout out and everybody swears and it's embarrassing. I wouldn't mind them speaking Punjabi but they go overboard and even when you do speak Punjabi, everybody else thinks you're talking about them. That's not fair. (SE)

SE's comments reveal the embarrassment experienced by the Rebels at the sight of Asian girls speaking their home languages in school. Such incidents reminded them of the 'difference' between themselves and white students. This was why, for example, so many of the Rebels were actively engaged in maintaining distinctions between themselves and the Gang girls.

> Well, I don't like the girls who are really like, 'Pakis', I know I'm a Paki, but at least I don't speak my own language in front of people. It sometimes embarrasses you in front of your mates. But I don't really bother about that now because the friends I'm hanging round with now, that's what they do and when you've got no one else you don't really bother. (AA)

Here a Muslim girl makes a distinction between being labelled Paki because of perceived membership of an Asian ethnic group and behaviour that is considered to be rude and embarrassing in the context of the wider culture of the school and, by implication, is more deserving of racial abuse. The articulation of such views not only gave strength to racist discourse but was central in the struggle to assert their identities as different to those of the Gang girls. The use of the racist term of abuse 'Paki' helped to further subjugate the Gang girls' femininity as backward and isolationist. Because they actively dissociated from the Gang girls, the attitudes and actions of the Rebels contrasted with those of the Gang girls, who were characterised as 'backward' or as 'refusing to integrate'.

The Rebels were not simply mimicking the mainstream; there was evidence of a fusion of languages emerging, with some girls speaking English and their home language in the same sentence. They could be interpreted thereby as creating new hybrid forms of linguistic and cultural expression. (Bhachu, 1991; Back, 1994).

> I don't really speak Punjabi at school. At the moment I've started speaking half Punjabi and half English to my friend [****]. My sister keeps picking on me about that. It's 'cause, she does it y'know, when I'm around and I pick things up but I wouldn't speak all Punjabi. (SJ)

Friendships

Friendship patterns were central to the struggle over different Asian femininities and illustrated various survival techniques. Embarrassed by what was perceived to be an 'all Asian girl gang mentality', five of the Rebels associated only with white students, avoiding other Asian people in the school. One described Asian girls as 'immature', and 'narrow minded', particularly where relationships or association with boys are concerned.

I speak to the Asian girls but I'm not 'pally' with them. My friends are white girls from nursery. The other Pakistani girls in my year, they're dead immature. They always laugh at boys when they go past. I just don't take any notice of them because I think they're a waste of time. (NS)

We saw that NS, a young Sikh girl, was encouraged by her father to 'integrate' by associating largely with white students. Another girl from an Islamic background took a similar stance:

I'd like to mix in with these Asian girls but 'em these girls are so narrow minded. Whatever their parents believe is hammered into them. So for that reason I don't really mix with them a lot. I prefer to hang around with Jewish and English girls ... Like in general conversation you say some things you don't really mean and they take it to heart. Like I go night-clubbing. One girl in my form she's very narrow-minded, Very! It was only yesterday she found I go to clubs and she still hasn't got over it! [Laughs]. (FH)

This illustrates again the Rebels' active role in reproducing dominant assumptions of Asian cultures as backward. These two girls were from different ethnic backgrounds (Indian Sikh and Pakistani Muslim) but both were from families that had originated from cities on the sub-continent rather than villages and their families had settled in the same region of Greater Manchester. The parents of the girls they spoke about were from rural backgrounds in Pakistan and currently lived in areas inhabited predominantly by Asians. Both girls adopt practices into their femininity associated with dominant white culture. These factors of region of origin and regional location in Britain cut across factors of religion and ethnicity. Their common neighbourhood in England and their parents' urban origin accounted for their shared experiences and perceptions at school (Bhachu, 1991).

For RH too, the urban/rural divide from back home was an important mechanism in producing a distinction between herself and other Asian girls. Although she shared a common class background with the girls, she seized on this distinction in order to justify maintaining her distance from other Asian girls in her school:

R H: I don't really talk to any of them [Asians].

FS: Why?

R H: I don't know. It's my parents really. My mum doesn't really get on with these people. They come from a different part of Pakistan, Mirpur, and my mum's from Lahore.

Academic progress and career aspirations

The girls in this category were located in the mid to higher sets and this too influenced their approach to schooling. Six stated their intentions of studying beyond compulsory schooling. One wished to study mathematics and languages, three were to study law. Others mentioned careers in psychiatry or medicine and one girl wished to join the police. All but two girls articulated their confidence and determination to succeed. Unlike the Gang girls, the majority of the Rebels had won the firm support of their families so were more confident about their career prospects. The comment of one girl was typical:

> I'm doing well. I'm confident, I want to do a combined Maths and languages degree, six months here, six months abroad ... I'll get financial and moral support form my parents and the school is very encouraging. (KP)
>
> FS: Do you see any obstacles in the way?
>
> KP: I've come over racial harassment, but I can deal with that. Sexual discrimination but I can deal with that. You have to doubly impress them really. Just give that bit more to prove you're as good as any man. I think I can do that.
>
> FS: Is it the same for racism?
>
> KP: It goes the same for racism. You have to prove that bit more because you're a woman and that bit more again because you're not white.

But two of the girls, SJ and FH, were less confident. They confessed that their progress had been hampered by their own activities such as associating with boys and going out to night-clubs, messing around and wasting time. These are also the characteristics associated with the rebel category. All were aware that the existence of racism could be an obstacle to their future careers.

> The general impression I get is it's more hard for Asian people to get into medicine and law, because of much more competition and when you're Asian, they look at you and they prefer whites, although they say they're not like that ... Just the white students really and the people of white origin because they'd be more preferred by high class white chairman/ person who would be sitting around the table deciding who they're going to enrol. (FH)

These Rebels, then, did not blame the family as the major obstacle to their future careers, so contradicting the dominant stereotypes of Asian family life. But two of the Rebels did see their family and the community surrounding them as the major block to their future career:

> They think women should stay at home and men should go out to work. That really makes me sick. In my family, my dad goes and wakes my mum to get him something to eat and it makes me angry. It's the same in my family but I've learned to look at it differently, but they haven't. Pakistani girls don't really want to go on. In our year, only three of the girls really want to make something of themselves and I hate the way Pakistani people are brought up. In my family I don't like the way they brought me up. Men are so chauvinist. And women are: [mimicking her mother] 'It's not a good thing boys cooking, it's a girl's job'! (SE)

Unlike the Gang girls, some of whom had similar experiences of family life, SE did not internalise the low expectations of Asian girls in society and spoke of her determination to succeed academically.

Racist name-calling

Despite associating with white girls and conforming to western notions of femininity, the girls were not altogether spared from name-calling. 'Black bitch', 'Paki' and 'go back to your own country' were among the main racist insults levelled at them. However their responses to this name-calling marked them out as different to the other girls. They were less likely than the Gang girls to respond defiantly.

Only two girls claimed that they had never been subjected to racist name-calling. Both of them dressed in western fashions and actively avoided other Asian girls and saw these as the reasons:

> I don't know really. Maybe it's because I don't hang round with the Asian girls. (FR)

> I think it's how you dress actually. None of them call me names, but the other girls walk past the boys call them. I think it's the way they dress mainly but they act a bit weird ... all joining together like in a big gang. It doesn't feel right. They don't mix in with the English. It's the way these Asian girls are that gets them called names, like all in a big gang and not mixing with the English. (RH)

This demonstrates awareness that 'hanging round with the English' is a way of avoiding being subjected to name-calling that was characteristic of the Survivors' strategy. RH felt that racism could be provoked by Asian girls themselves. This view was shared by SE who said:

> I think sometimes it's their own fault. Pakistani ladies, they don't really know how to control their children. [It was] seven a.m. the other day, a Pakistani lad in the street completely naked and his mum doesn't care. They think it's Pakistan. When English people stare, I don't blame them.

A distinction was made between 'ordinary white students' and a 'rough' element, whom they cited as the main 'troublemakers' in the school. So apparently the Rebels did not view all white people as 'the enemy' the way the Gang girls did. When subjected to racist name-calling, the Rebels were less likely than the Gang girls to act defiantly and less inclined to protect other Asian students from abuse. There were two main reasons for this: they felt insecure because they did not have the support of the Asian girl groups but, more importantly, because of their more positive relations with teachers, they felt more able to report such incidents to teachers, as reported here:

> In the first year we were queuing up for dinner. The dinner ladies had numbered us. A girl came up and said, 'Don't tell anyone, you Paki'. I burst into tears and told the dinner lady who reprimanded her and took it to the deputy head Mrs [****]. Between us, we sorted it out. I think she learned from it. The colour of my skin doesn't make a difference. You do get people in the street, yobbos basically, calling you 'Paki' but you learn to ignore it because they're just ignorant. I'm not bothered by it. If it was one of my friends I would be. (KP)

How the school dealt with racism in this particular case was significant. Because of an institutional policy to deal actively and immediately with racist incidents, KP felt able to report the incident to a member of staff in the knowledge that it would be promptly dealt with. But possibly too, it was because she was a Rebel that she was believed. As we saw, some of the Gang girls reported that such requests for assistance were ignored and not acted upon or that they were actively disbelieved. Another example of such distinctions between Rebels and Gang girls as 'deserving' and 'non-deserving' can be seen here in the context of racist name-calling:

> SE: Some [students] in the higher sets I know call people names too and when I hear them they turn around and say 'sorry! It's no offence to you'.
>
> FS: What do you feel then?
>
> SE: I feel like smacking them in the mouth and I tell them 'how can it be no offence to me when they're Muslims. I'm Muslim. If they're Pakis I must

be a Paki'. I tell them and they just say 'sorry it was no offence'. But it does offend me. It's mostly boys, only a couple of girls, they're really nice to us but with other people they're awful.

Although SE does not collude in the racism, the example illustrates that a strategy of keeping a distance from the Gang girls works to position the Rebels as the exceptions to the rule. But the racist attitudes of white students are nonetheless maintained.

Sexist name-calling
The dissociation from the Asian girl gangs may have helped the Rebels in the higher sets to avoid racist name-calling but their willingness to associate with boys and to be involved in romantic relations made them vulnerable to sexist name-calling. So they were likely to be subjected to sexist name-calling as well as the disapproval of other Asian girls because they associated with boys.

Three were involved in heterosexual relationships – all without the knowledge of their parents. Resistance against parental expectations was therefore covert rather than overt. All were outspoken on the issue of relations with the opposite sex. One was particularly critical of her parents and her comment appears to feed into the common-sense racist notion that Asian cultures are 'backward'.

I don't agree. This is a more permissive society than where my mum and dad were brought up so I feel they're putting their backward thoughts onto me. (KP)

A major characteristic of the Rebels, then, was that even though they found romantic relationships acceptable, the way they handled them showed little evidence of overt resistance. They hid their relationships from parents. As one girl told me:

I think if you like somebody you should say so, [but] not to [your] parents because they'd shuffle you off to Pakistan. So I tell friends who don't make a big deal. (SE)

This highlights the girls' fears lest overt resistance would end their academic careers and at worst could lead to their being sent back to the subcontinent.

They were also excluded or disapproved of for adopting a western image. FH was a particular target of the Gang girls in her school, who frequently referred to her as 'slag' or 'tart'.

FS: Have you ever been called any names?

FH: 'Tart' by other Asian girls. I'm not bothered. It's because they can't do it [go to night-clubs and dress in western fashions]. If they could they'd understand. We just laugh at them and make them paranoid.

FH admitted visiting night-clubs without her parents' permission but firmly believed that her father had some idea of this, since he frequently collected her in the early hours of the morning. Although she regularly went to night-clubs she rejected Asian bhangras because she thought that 'too many childish lads' attended them. In another school, SJ was also labelled a tart.

Well, last year I used to be like – I know myself I used to dress to like a bit of a tart and have a mini-skirt and people used to call me 'tart' but I wasn't bothered about it ... I never used to say anything. I used to give them dirty looks and all that. My friends used to say it's because they're jealous 'cause you're allowed to do this and they're not because most of the English girls weren't allowed to do it. (SJ)

Lees (1997) has argued that one of the difficulties for girls subjected to such labelling is the incontestable nature of the term slag. The two girls however draw on the racialised discourses of femininity to argue that the other Asian girls are jealous of the freedom they experience.

Family

Family life was varied, and cut across differences of religion. The traditional father figure was present in most families, but two girls spoke about a dominant mother. As one said:

My dad .. always goes along with her. Like if she says 'don't give her [me] any money', he doesn't, but when she turns her back he gives me money then he says, 'don't tell your mum I've given to you'. It's like he's frightened of her. (SE)

The responses of the Rebels were not categorically defined as resistance against culture because most (six) made positive comments about their family experiences. KP and FH spoke of the encouragement they received from their families, particularly in terms of support for their careers and further education. Only two girls were extremely critical of their parents (particularly their mothers) and claimed to receive very little support from them. Despite speaking positively about their family experiences, these girls were significantly more likely to identify unequal gender relations in the family and community as the major cause of their oppression. This is clearly illustrated in the following response:

> RE: Whenever I do lessons, I get homework. My mum and dad don't help me. If it was my brother, my mum and dad would, but not me and my sisters. They just say, 'you can do it yourself' and they say, 'I can't help you, I haven't got time' and if my mum wants us to make chapatis and we've got a lot of homework to do she always brags about it.
>
> FS: Brags?
>
> RE: To everybody. She doesn't even know, 'Girls aren't good enough', She goes, 'If I had the chance to choose whether I had boys or girls I'd rather have boys'.

It was her definition of family experience that influenced the girl's attitudes towards school, which she regarded as a positive experience, and it also affected her dissociation from other Asian girls in the school.

Religion
The girls in this category came from two different religious backgrounds: Islam and Sikhism. All the girls identified religion as important, but it was important in different ways, in particular, as a guide rather than a prescriptive code for behaviour. The girls did not passively accept religious teachings passed on to them by parents or by religious teachers. Instead, an active negotiation process was in evidence in terms of the religious aspects they considered acceptable or unacceptable. In the process new religious identities were being created.

> We're not strict Muslims. I believe in the main ideas – decency, not mixing with boys and covering yourself. That's why I do wear salwar-kameez. I feel comfortable. I wear trousers to cover my legs. I don't judge other people who wear skirts. It's my decision to cover my legs. My mum tells me things ... stories ... from the *Quoran*. I find it interesting what you're supposed to do compared to what people actually do e.g. burial. I like to hear so that I can make up my own mind. (KP)

She stated that she disapproved of sex before marriage and believed it was the worst imaginable sin. She did not, however, identify any problems with associating or having relationships with boys. Another girl expressed a similarly ambivalent attitude:

> It's er .. I don't know. No, yes and no. It's important. I do keep to some rules, eating *halal* meat, I don't drink, premarital sex and all that lot, but

em, I've not really thought about it. I just live each day as it comes and do what I feel like. I feel guilty sometimes. (FH)

For FH, too, the issue of romantic relationships was the main point of departure from religious teachings. However, rather significantly, her choice of partner was also constrained by religion (although she used the term Asian rather than Muslim to describe him). Religious ideas, then, had become adapted in these responses to suit the lifestyles of the girls within their regional locations.

FS: You implied earlier that you have a boyfriend?

FH: ...Yeah I am going out with someone, Asian, he's Asian. I still prefer to go out with Asians.

FS: Why is that?

FH: I don't think I'd go out with, well no. I have been out with whites. Even though I don't like to hang round with them. I just prefer to stick to my own. Its not being racist or anything. I just feel more comfortable. I'd feel I had more in common. He's Muslim. I'd never go out with a Hindu or Sikh, they eat pork [laughs].

A young Sikh woman also identified religion as important to her, and found she was more likely to conform when in contact other people of the same religion, which demonstrated her commitment to context appropriate behaviour.

It does when I'm around other people of the same religion, because if I don't act like they expect, they think low of you ... I behave in the way [that] they think is right. (NS)

Initially, the following response appears to support the cultural pathology discourse. However, as RE continued to talk, it emerged that she had made a clear distinction between religion and custom, thereby challenging the findings of Rashid (1981), and this distinction was also made by other girls. When asked whether religion was important to her, she replied:

No! I hate being a Muslim! I do like being a Muslim but it says in the Quoran you shouldn't have to get married against your will but my mum she made up her own religion. All my relatives go round telling everyone what's wrong and right. She lets us wear nail polish and make-up but sometimes in front of people she says 'Why are you wearing nail polish? Take it off!' She just changes. She makes her own rules because our Imam says you can wear make-up as long as it hasn't got animal fat in it. (RE)

The distinction between religion and custom is also apparent in SE's response:

> It's not the religion. I think the religion is good It's just the people. it's their tradition they think about more than the religion. Like my dad even though he's a *Molbi* [teacher of the *Quoran*], he still thinks more about his tradition and this community. They make their own rules. he says 'do this or that, if you're a Muslim you'll do it'. I say, 'it's nothing to do with [being a] Muslim' and I have to say it because I've studied it all, because of my sister. (SE)

The issue of involvement with boys was a common point of departure for the Rebels from their commitment to religious teachings. Religion was nonetheless identified as important and not necessarily as a restrictive force in their lives.

> Well, it's important but there's some things about my religion that I don't believe in like the way you're supposed to dress, who you're allowed to talk to. It's stupid, I think, but like I read the *Quoran* every day so I am pretty religious. (SJ)

> NP: Sometimes it is important but sometimes it isn't 'cause you feel that you want to do this thing and you want to leave religion out of it, but sometimes you have to put religion in. You have to think about it before you do something.

> FS: Can you give me an example of when you wanted to do something and you've stopped?

> NP: Like go out with boys y'know. Then you think, oh, you shouldn't be doing this but you do it and you want to do it and if your parents find out they start moaning. They do and then take you to Pakistan. That's what normally happens, but not in our family.

Future aspirations

With the exception of two girls, all the Rebels were optimistic about the future, and none indicated that they would voluntarily place marriage before a career, as the Gang girls or the Faith girls said they would. Five stated that they would be willing to marry out of their religious group, the highest in the sample, and four said that they might never marry. Three definitely saw themselves as getting married and only two saw themselves unwillingly in marriages. Although there are obvious problems associated with a reliance on future predictions, this does indicate that not all the girls despaired about the prospect of the future. This clearly contradicts the cultural pathology argument according to which young Asian women are 'helpless little creatures', living in fear of arranged marriages. Only two of the Rebels feared such a marriage and one described her feelings thus:

> SE: I want to think I'll be a big lawyer but really, deep down I think I'll be sitting at home crying because I don't think my parents will let me go. But if anyone asks me, I say,' Oh yeah I'm going to be a big lawyer' but really, I know I'm going to be sitting at home like my sister.
>
> FS: Married?
>
> SE: Yes, definitely. I already know who I'm going to get married to because my mum wants her nephews to come here.

I categorise as 'Rebel' this girl's response, primarily because she did not actively resist nor did she accept the inevitability of a future role as only wife and mother. She identified education as important for her and as her 'way out'. She also asserted that she would continue to adopt a survival strategy in the hope that she might be allowed to pursue her goals of academic success and thereby secure a form of independence.

> Education is the most important thing to me ... I've always said that if they want to get me married (if they allow me to go on) then I would and if I wasn't happy I would get a divorce but that's out of the question ... but I would. (SE)

The consequences of being a Rebel

A major characteristic of the Rebels' approach was deferred gratification. However on occasion, at least three of the girls appeared to seek immediate gratification. This included 'going out', having romantic relationships and night-clubbing – all of which had caused problems for their studies. The girls were extremely confident about their abilities and most expected to be academically successful.

As a result of adopting a survival strategy that involved dissociating themselves from Asian girl gangs and seeking out white friendships, they were accepted in the school and 'liked' by white students and staff alike. However, the Gang girls disliked them, seeing them as being incorporated into white society and as collaborating in their racial oppression in the school. They were particularly disliked for their adoption of a western image and for their association with boys in the schools.

The girls were actively encouraged to succeed academically by staff, who spoke of them favourably and sometimes referred to them as 'Rebels', applying the term positively. Intriguingly, it was not used to describe the Gang girls, who, as we have seen, were labelled as trouble-makers by staff in the schools. In some situations, the Rebels actively reinforced negative stereotyping of Asians precisely because their willingness to mix, dress in western clothes and go to night-clubs allowed them to be viewed as exceptions to the rule that Asian girls do not integrate. Their behaviour was contrasted with an abiding image of a 'gang' of Pakistanis who, by comparison with the Rebels, seemed even more resistant to integrating.

The Rebels were playing an active role in the transformation of their cultures, and this has long term implications for future Asian cultures. They were involved in transforming aspects of their social conditions, such as religious practices, by rejecting some aspects but retaining others. By rejecting particular aspects of religious and cultural teach-ings, however, they may be reinforcing the stereotyped notion that Asian cultures operate 'backward' practices.

7
The Faith Girls

The girls in this category – the 'Faith girls' – drew on a combination of the resistance through culture (Gang girls) and Survival strategies. What differentiated their responses from those of the Gang girls was their pursuit of academic success while in school and their relatively more positive relations with staff and students. Their prioritisation of racism as the main source of oppression within the school was the factor that distinguished their responses from those of the Survivors, but this group identified themselves primarily by their religion (Muslim, Sikh or Hindu) rather than ethnic group (Pakistani or Indian).

The Faith girls demonstrated an experiential understanding of racism but did not resist by associating with the Asian girl gangs. They were predominantly in mid and high sets, where there were fewer Asian pupils with whom to form such alliances. They generally conformed to the concept of the good pupil by working hard to achieve academic success and abiding by school rules. They were nevertheless subjected to racist name-calling because of their cultural or religious identification and views but were less likely to retaliate physically. Their active resistance was rare and the reason was primarily to defend a principle (usually concerned with religion). For example, one young Sikh woman believed that it was the hypocrisy she perceived in other students (mainly Muslims) in the school that was the source of her frustration. She describes her disappointment with these students for ridiculing her brother's choice to wear a turban:

> I said, 'if you don't want to wear things that represent your religion it's fine, but if he does, just let him. It was mainly Muslim people. I said, 'you wear white hats to mosque, why don't you wear them to school. If he

goes to the Gurdwara he wears his turban and he also wears it to school. He's proud to be a Sikh. Why don't you be proud to be a Muslim?' (BS)

Schooling is an important site for the contestation of ethnic identities in relation to the hegemonic white culture of the school. The turban is a highly visible symbol of non-conformity and here Muslim students (predominantly male), both by their negative comments and by not wearing their hats (marking their Muslim identity) into school actively contribute to the marginalisation and subordination of these identities. The girls were involved in an active struggle to defend their religious identities and were therefore prepared to speak out on issues that challenged them but otherwise they presented conformity to the dominant stereotype of the shy, timid and passive Asian girl.

Teachers

The majority of the girls managed positive relations with staff because they apparently conformed to the dominant stereotypes and because they did not associate with girl gangs – although they did not actively dissociate themselves from them either. This was related to their being in the higher sets. Three of the girls identified the teachers as 'kind' and 'encouraging':

> It's a good school, they try to keep bad experiences out. There are some rough girls but that's going to happen in any school. It's a friendly school, the teachers are nice. It's a developing school and teachers have good ideas too. (YB)

Only two of the girls said that they would not go to a white teacher if they had a problem. One stated that this was because of teachers' assumptions that every Asian girl would have an arranged marriage. While their relationships with teachers were positive, the girls did not turn a blind eye to incidents or actions or practices involving teachers they identified as racist. They were alert to institutional racism, as highlighted by the marginalisation of Islamic religious values, and to 'colour' racism:

> Sometimes it really gets to me and I get worked up. Well, it's like ... I don't know. When they don't understand that you can't do certain things like in Islam. I don't know if it's true or anything but what I've heard is that you can't draw pictures like of people because when you do, you have to put Jaan [life] in it right. But they don't understand that and they make you do it. It bugs me so I get a short temper. I get really mad. ...If I answer back

to 'em, I'll get into trouble and the teacher, my form teacher, before he had an accident, we used to have an argument every single day. I mean like 'Take your coat off!', 'Put your chair in.' The more he said it, the more it made me not want to do it, so it really got on my nerves. Like once, it's so funny this, right, I was talking to my friend, and I was positioned like this [legs to side of table] and sir told me to put my legs under and so I turned round but I didn't really put my legs under. Well, I guess I did it on purpose, y'know to get on his nerves, but then I put my legs under the table and then when I turned round I put my legs back and he said, 'Right, you're going to stay behind at dinner '. And they make you do stupid things like make you write a letter saying why you have to put your legs under the table. And you just write anything down. It bugs me sometimes. It just gets on your nerves. Then like, he knows that and like, I talk a lot, but I do all my work and everything. (TT)

The frustration of this girl seems to stem from having to take part in activities that directly challenge religious requirements. Like the Gang girls, TT responds by directly opposing existing school rules but, unlike them, it is religion that drives her to resist the teacher's authority. Her response to some extent corresponds with the findings of Fuller (1983) and Mac an Ghaill (1988) because despite being opposed to schooling, TT was pro-education and teachers found her work satisfactory. The second example illustrates a different racism (Goldberg, 1990) and also the contradictory nature of racism itself, in that racist discourse that relies on the construction of biological difference coexists with cultural and religious racism.

PB: Some teachers are racist over our colour. The deputy head Mr [****], he's racist, because I remember I had fight with an English girl and she hit me, but I didn't hit her back. I told the teacher that I could have hit her back because she was younger than me, but didn't. I went and told the teacher about this and he said he'd do something about it and the girl just left so he couldn't do anything about it. But then again he could have done something about it then and there, but he didn't. He could have suspended her because she punched me in my eye with her nail and it poked my eye and I had to have a bandage over my eye for two to three weeks.

FS: How did you feel?

PB: I felt really embarrassed because when my friends asked me why I didn't hit her back, but because she was younger ... and ... she was white the teacher took her side instead of mine, I didn't like the way he acted. He told me to go to my lesson and he would talk to her but he didn't because whenever she passed me she said, 'served you right' and told all her friends.' Oh you went and told sir but he didn't do anything about did he?' That's what really got me. If I'd been an English girl he would have done something.

Rather that drawing on a female network as the Gang girls do, PB chose to tell a teacher but she was extremely disappointed with the outcome. Her teacher's failure to act confirmed her view of him as racist. She had no doubt that had she been 'English', the teacher would have supported her. On another occasion, the teacher reprimanded the girl and her friends for allegedly betting in class over a cricket match.

Once we were just mucking about and pretending to have a bet on cricket. We weren't even going to take the money off him and were doing it for a laugh but he told us off. He also said Pakistan cheated [in the 1992 World cup]. (PB)

Gambling or betting in school is against school rules and so the teacher had cause to reprimand them. However, it is PB's last sentence that is so revealing of the ways in which wider discourses on race impact on specific and sometimes harsh punishments applied to Asian students. Rather than ignoring the incident as a joke, as the students claimed it was, the teacher chooses to treat it seriously. In doing so he draws on the reference to the cheating in the world cup cricket series of 1992, where Pakistani cricketers playing England were labelled as 'cheats' and 'hot-heads' in the ball-tampering controversy. As Searle (1993) notes, this controversy has had a significant impact on schooling experiences, drawing as it does on common-sense racist imagery rooted in Britain's imperial past of Asians as sly. The incident reported by PB suggests that these dominant stereotypical images of Asians and particularly Pakistani men informed common-sense assumptions in the school which directly affected young Asian women students. PB was dis-believed on two occasions by a member of staff whose approach indicated his ready acceptance of assumptions that Asians are sly and untrustworthy.

Disappointment of this nature with the attitudes of mainstream white teachers led the Gang girls to request the employment of Asian teachers in the school but the Faith girls did not necessarily see this appropriate.

Asian teachers

Half the Faith girls (i.e. four) did not wish to see more Asian teachers in the school while the other half said they would. They gave various reasons. The reason given by one corresponded with that of the Gang girls – that is, assumed shared cultural and religious identity with Asian teachers. This was referred to earlier as 'the burden of representation' (Parmar, 1990), whereby Asian teachers are expected to act on behalf of Asian students in the school even if they have different priorities and concerns.

> Yes, because they'd be able to understand you more than the [white] teachers. (AS)

> I'd like to see them teach English because it would be more easy for the Asian people to understand and I think Asian people would be glad as well. (AB)

> Yeah if they can handle it. I mean, they [white pupils] take advantage of them [Asian teachers], if they're a different colour. English people think they can say anything and get away with it. Even the Asians swear in front of them and they don't say anything. (TT)

These responses are revealing about the marginal status of Asian teachers. This is evident in the students' use of 'the teachers' to refer to white teachers. The second response reflects the assumption that they teach languages rather than mainstream subjects. In the third example, rather than viewing Asian teachers as 'incompetent', the focus is the problems these teacher face from white students. This implies recognition of the internalisation of racism by Asian students, that is, they too were perceived to respond like 'the English' by not viewing Asians as 'real' teachers and not taking them seriously in the classroom. PB demonstrated her understanding of structural racism when she highlighted the systematic exclusion of Asian teachers:

> They don't really put Asian teachers in school anyway. Then again, we wanted a new Asian teacher for Urdu but they gave us an English teacher and all she does is give us leaflets and tell us to copy them out . . they could have got a supply teacher, another Urdu teacher free. We asked the head but she didn't do anything. Finally we got her. We have to fight for our rights. (PB)

Her reason for wanting more Asian teachers was that they could provide positive role models. She believed that Asian teachers who dressed in a traditional manner enabled Asian students to 'feel like more yourself'. Clearly however, this places a burden upon Asian teachers, generally women, who might not wish to wear traditional dress.

Academic progress and future aspirations

The Faith girls were predominantly found in the mid to high sets. When they spoke of their definite career plans, it appeared that three girls wished to study medicine and others named, law, pharmacy, electronics or engineering. The choices thus confirmed the findings of Singh (1991) that these are the most popular subject choices for Asian students in higher education institutions. Only two girls mentioned non-academic careers as options: one wanted to be a receptionist in a doctor's surgery and the other wished to work in a knitting factory.

The Faith girls were likely to identify sexism and racism as obstacles to their careers.

> YB: Perhaps being a girl might make it harder but that's changing all the time. By the time I get there it will be easier.

> KS: There's not a lot of women in physics and engineering.

> FS: Will there be obstacles?

> KS: I'd like to think that colour doesn't matter but I don't really know ... I've had the impression that nobody's prejudiced but I think there's bound to be. If I work hard hopefully they'll think of that above everything else.

Despite their awareness of structural racism and sexism and their apparent confidence about going to university, four of the girls who expressed a wish to do so ultimately accepted that they would instead be married and would not achieve their chosen careers. One Muslim girl justified this as follows:

> Actually, I wouldn't mind staying at home to have kids. I don't know if it would get boring after a few years and it's more difficult to get back into work, I've heard anyway. I think I'd like a job. Something in electronics, but I don't want too much of a pressured job that's on my mind twenty-four hours a day and I can't have my life outside work. I don't know if I could cope with bringing up kids and having a job like that but I'd like to try. (KS)

This was not restricted to the experience of Muslims: one Sikh Indian girl who had expressed a desire to be a pharmacist also said:

> I might have to get married at 21. It's the way, so I won't make it to university. Maybe [to] college. (BS)

This illustrates an acceptance of uneven gender patterns within the household, which here cut across the factor of religion. However, unlike the Gang girls, the Faith girls did not give up in school but continued to work in the hope that they might eventually be allowed to have a career. So we see a combination of survival and resistance through culture (Gang girls) in their responses. The perceived religious and cultural requirements overshadowed the need to succeed academically, beyond compulsory schooling. This combination of survival and resistance through culture is encapsulated in the response of one of the Faith girls:

> TT: I want to do something in medicine ... I'm in the top sets and I want to try for Oxford or Cambridge.
>
> FS: Will there be any obstacles?
>
> TT: My mum would want me to get married at 22. My brother says 'what are you going to do? Are you going to do what your mum says and get married? I say, ' I'm probably going to get married to my education first because at least if something goes wrong, I'll be able to have my own job and earn my own money'. That's what my dad [recently deceased] wanted.

TT thus adopts a survival approach, prioritising academic success. On other occasions, her views corresponded to the resistance through culture approach adopted by the Gang girls:

> Sometimes I feel I just don't care. What's the point of doing my GCSE's, I might as well sit at home. (TT)

Family

The girls spoke positively about their families but on occasion identified pressures on them in the home. Talking of her father, KS remarks:

> Sometimes I think he goes on a bit, I get the feeling sometimes, he doesn't trust us but even when I've not done anything wrong, he seems to imply he doesn't trust us. (KS)

Despite a few such comments, the girls generally tried to justify parental wishes by being supportive of them. This was evident in the way key decisions such as choice of marriage partner were willingly left to parents.

Dress

Four of the Faith girls wore traditional dress; three of them claiming this to be of their own choosing. They thus displayed willing conformity to traditional requirements, except for the one girl who conformed un-willingly (Drury, 1991). A further three girls wore both traditional and western clothing, which they claimed was of their own choosing. Only one girl wore a head-scarf – reluctantly.

> [I wear] salwar-kameez, I am allowed to wear trousers in school and on trips but my mum thinks all other Asians will probably think, look at her, but on our street there are no Asians. [They are] all white and we get on. (TT)

Dress can be extremely important symbol of resistance to either tradi-tional religious and cultural values or western values. The wearing of *hijab* has been particularly controversial issue in contemporary western societies. In the autumn of 1994 a 13 year old Muslim girl at a French school in Montreal was sent home on grounds that the scarf she was wearing did not conform to the school's dress code. Similar struggles have taken place elsewhere in Canada. The *Times Educational Supplement* of 27 January 1995 reported that Franscois Lemieux, head of the nationalist St Jean Baptiste Society was quoted as saying that *hijab* is incompatible with the values of Quebec society because it 'defies the values of equality of men and women that we have in Quebec'. However Edward Broadbent, former leader of Canada's socialist-leaning New Democratic Party demanded:

> How can we possibly deny the right to wear *hijab* here and defend the right of women not to wear the *hijab* in Muslim Countries? (ibid)

In Turkey too, women students in *hijab* were not permitted to be taught on university campuses. It remains to be seen what changes the govern-ment of the Islamic party elected in November 2002 will make with regard to this issue. In post-Taliban Afghanistan there were discussions about whether Afghani women would abandon the *hijab* as an early sign that the country had been liberated.

One student who wore full *hijab* did not wish to comment on it as in any way unusual:

> My dad is quite religious. He tells us everything. I wear *hijab* outside school. When I go to college, I will [too]. My dad talks to us about that. Sometimes I think he goes on a bit. (KS)

She also wore traditional dress as part of *hijab*, arguing:

> I prefer salwar-kameez. I don't want to loose touch with my culture but I'd like some western clothes for a change, but I do prefer salwar-kameez personally. (KS)

Three of the Faith girls claimed they willingly wore traditional clothes and – characteristically – that it was of their own choosing. They offered various practical reasons as justification.

> I've grown out of wearing skirts and dresses. I'm allowed it, but I've grown out of it. I wear trousers, jeans and salwar-kameez. I feel comfortable because in summer time you want to wear something cool instead of trousers. (BS)

However, unwilling conformity was found in the following response:

> AS: Salwar-kameez, [is] not my choice, I have to. If I had a choice I would wear trousers. I think it's because my mum's friend ... her daughter used to wear trousers. They went out with people and ran away and now my mum says, 'don't wear trousers'. My mum thinks if you wear trousers and act like English people you might do that.
>
> FS : What do you think?
>
> AS: I think, just because the person does it doesn't mean everyone will. You might say you're not going to do it but when you get there you might.

Language

Only two of the Faith girls used their home language in school as a mechanism for exclusion (Wright, 1992; Mac An Ghaill, 1988).

> I speak Punjabi and Urdu with cousins and sometimes in school with my mates. Well, some people say 'what did you say just now?' And they carry on just talking. 'This girl told me this thing', what does it mean and we have to tell them what them it means like. They know more than us now. (AB)

> I sometimes use Punjabi with friends at school. Sometimes some English people say, 'what are you saying' because they don't understand. I don't tell them anything. Sometimes we call them names and they don't know what we're talking about. (AS)

The other six girls in this group did not use language as a weapon, and conformed to the survival response of language in school. Home language was only spoken in situations where required, for example when helping a student with language difficulties. Two claimed that they would not be ashamed to use their home language in school.

> YB: If I had to, I would. I'm not ashamed or anything – but not unnecessarily, like people who go around who can speak English. People think if you speak your own language then you're speaking about them.

> TT: I speak Punjabi a bit.

> FS: In school?

> TT: No, I'm embarrassed. It feels different.

Although TT disobeyed her form teacher in school she did not use language as a mechanism of exclusion.

Friends

All the Faith girls chose to associate with friends from different backgrounds but confessed to associating or identifying mainly with other Asian girls (most of them from within their own religious group). This was true both in school and out. They particularly avoided 'racists' and 'trouble makers'. That they were seen in school to integrate with white students could be one explanation for their favourable treatment by teachers.

> YB: I only don't mix with people because of their attitude maybe to Asians people or just to other people. There are some rough girls sometimes friendly other times not. They make racist remarks. [...] They don't really mean it. It's just petty things. They don't hurt anybody but silly little remarks make a difference.

> FF: Well, the majority of my friends are English obviously, but I talk to Asian girls and I come to school and I leave school with Asians. I see those girls out of school as well, but I mainly talk to English girls in school. I don't really see them out of school.

> FS: How come you mix mainly with English girls here?

> FF: I don't know. It's because there's more English girls in my classes, there's not a lot of Asians. I just get on with everyone.

Their comments echo an important characteristic of the Survivors: adopting what they considered appropriate behaviour in relation to friendship patterns.

Boys

The Rebels defied religious and cultural requirements concerning mixing with boys, whereas the Gang girls complied with them. The Faith girls neither involved themselves in romantic relationships, nor were they critical or judgmental of those who did. YB, for example, said:

> It's up to them. I don't think it's right. Behind their parents' back either. [I'm] not thinking of being a Muslim, I mean behind their parents' – but it's up to them ... You can be friends but not as in boyfriend and girlfriend. That's religion and me and I've been brought up like that . . but I don't think it's that shocking.

One girl was extremely cautious about associating with the opposite sex because her father appeared to be highly suspicious of her behaviour in ordinary circumstances. The implication was that the risk of being caught was far too high for her even to consider taking part in any activities involving boys. This also appears to have been what hindered AB:

> Well, you've got to get caught one day I would say but if you like your cousin it's different. [It's] like I like my cousin but I haven't the guts to say it to my parents. They're too strict. I don't know what to do.

Only one of the girls in this category mixed with the opposite sex and she had permission from her parents – but only because they trusted her not to become romantically involved.

> My parents are okay about me mixing with boys. They know I won't do anything stupid. (BS)

Two Faith girls echoed Survivors in their comments about the apparent immaturity of Asian boys in the school. According to them, this made the mixing of the sexes extremely difficult.

> The English don't mind sitting with a girl but Pakistanis, they're the worst of all because if they sit next to English girls they just move their chair and say I'm not sitting next to her, she's white and even if they do the rest will say, 'Oh she's sat next to Tariq, I wonder what's happening'. That's what I hate about Pakistanis. (PB)

> I don't like mixing with boys because if you do anything wrong, Pakistani boys start laughing and make fun of you.

Name-calling

All eight girls had been subjected to racist name-calling in one form or another. However, unlike the Gang girls, they were less likely to employ physical resistance – only two confessed to being involved in fighting after being verbally abused. Unlike the Rebels, they did not encounter sexist name-calling because they avoided being see with boys. Racist name-calling was accepted as part of their everyday experiences in schooling and society and they continued work towards their goal of academic success. However, as we have seen, they were more likely than the Survivors to act defiantly when their religion was perceived to be under attack. Six of the Faith girls stated that they would retaliate in some form or another but they avoided fighting as much as possible. Resistance was restricted to verbal responses, for example calling white students 'ice-cream face' in response to 'Paki' or 'black bitch'. Other girls adopted a much tighter survival strategy.

> I should say something back but if you say something, they just say something back and you get stuck in a position. (YB)

> I'm not bothered because everybody's always saying it [Paki] so what's the point in getting depressed about it. (AS)

Religion

Of all the girls who took part in the study, religion appeared to play the most important part in the daily lives of this group of girls. At least four identified themselves by their religious rather than ethnic group (as Muslim rather than Asian or Pakistani). Many referred interchangeably to 'Christians', 'whites' and 'the English', confirming that identity is not fixed but constantly re-positioned (Parmar, 1990; Hall, 1992; Mani and Frankenburg, 1993). Religion was identified as important in the following ways:

> It's important, the way I dress – my attitudes really. It's everyday life, the food I eat, the clothes I wear, my thoughts ... Christian girls have boy-friends and drink. I wouldn't because of my religion. I'm not practising but I still think of myself as Muslim and follow beliefs. (YB)

A Sikh Indian girl identified positively as Sikh and consistently identified other girls in the school by their religious rather than ethnic group.

> I've never done anything against my religion. I try to obey my religion – not cutting hair, not eating meat. But people say you mix with Muslim boys

– that doesn't bother me. I wouldn't go out with one .. Muslim girls look at me differently like, 'why do you mix with boys?' They stay away from me. (BS)

These comments reveal that the girls did not merely replicate their cultures, but that residual elements of religious identities were drawn on and reinterpreted to produce new religious identifications.

Future aspirations

We saw that when talking about their careers some girls 'chose' to forfeit their academic success goals because of parental expectations. Four expected to be married and have no careers. Three hoped they might have a career and all expected to be married. Marriage was not viewed a repressive inevitability. Again contrary to the stereotyped notions, they did not live in fear of arranged marriages. Indeed one girl defended the arranged marriage system in the following way:

Probably arranged, but I don't mind. I think there are good things in that too. Your parents get to know the other person and it's not just looks. It's qualification, personality and their family. There's marriages you can choose yourself, that won't work out so it's not all bad arranged. (YB)

Contrary to dominant discourses, the Faith girls did not feel that they were going to be forced into a loveless marriage and none indicated that they wished to marry outside their religious group. The girls quite obviously did not live in fear of arranged marriages.

I'll be married. [I'll be] in a house maybe of my own maybe [with] my in-laws, hopefully a job I could carry on or maybe a secretary. Mum and dad would choose a few people I could meet them. I'm confident that my mum and dad will choose well. He'll have a nice home – I'm not scared of being thrown into prison like cousins. He would have to be an Indian Sikh. (BS)

I don't have faith in my own judgement. I think I would take someone at face value. I can't make a decision like that. I'd prefer my mum and dad to choose but I'd still like my own choice. I'd rather my mum and dad picked him out then I'd also have my mum and dad's blessing. (FF)

Like these two girls, most of the Faith group spoke positively about their futures, which they saw as assured by their good relationships with their parents.

The consequences of being a Faith girl

Deferred gratification was an important feature of the Faith girls' behaviour. The girls did not join the all-Asian girl groups although they had some Asian friendships; they did not deliberately break school rules; nor did they involve themselves in romantic relationships, in pursuit of enjoyment. Instead, they worked conscientiously to achieve their academic goals. They thought it possible that they would continue with their studies – but only if their parents were agreeable. This could partly be explained by their location in the higher sets. They also enjoyed positive relations with staff and other students. The key factor in their peer relationships was their identification in terms of religion rather than ethnicity. As with all the Survivors and contrary to the Gang girls, these girls identified themselves as having positive relationships with staff. They were also viewed in a positive light in the school. It could be argued that positive relations with staff resulted from two things: first, because they were seen to mix with white students in school and second, because they appeared to conform to the stereotypes of quiet, meek Asian girls. Appearing to integrate with white students and not resisting teachers' authority may explain why they were encouraged to do well at school and were so confident about their ability to succeed academically.

However, these girls tended to talk about sacrificing career expectations for marriage, and they seemed willing to do so. They held onto the possibility that they might be able to combine marriage with a career. Despite expectations of marriage and motherhood, the girls continued to work conscientiously in school. They did not associate with the girl gangs, so the teachers and other students responded far more favourably to them. Like the girls described in the research of Shaw (1989) and Mirza (1988), the Faith girls identified positively with religion and this shaped their experiences in school.

Although the girls appeared to conform to the timid, shy and passive stereotypes, they were actively creating positive identities for themselves through religion. They drew on residual elements of their respective religious cultures and reworked them in the English context so that they operated in their favour.

8
Conclusion

The previous four chapters revealed the strategies Asian girls employed to deal with their schooling. Each chapter ended with a consideration of some of the consequences of each strategy they used. This chapter offers an overall conclusion and focuses on two main themes that have emerged that have practical implications for schooling.

The cultural pathology discourse, despite much criticism, remains a powerful and central reference point in popular conceptions of Asian family life and femininity in the UK. This discourse positions Asian girls as the victims of oppressive cultures in which men dominate women. Asian girls are characterised as caught between the two worlds of home, where they are restricted, and school, where they experience freedom. Public discussions in the aftermath of inner-city disturbances of 2001 and the events of September 11, 2001 have further reinforced characterisations of the poorest Asian communities, the Pakistani and Bangladeshi Muslims, as isolationist and refusing to integrate. These communities have been accused of holding onto backward and barbarous practices that prevent girls from partaking in mainstream activities and encourage boys to take up dangerous and fanatical positions.

I have shown that schooling plays a central role in filtering such discourses and is a site where wider relations of power and cultural definitions are both reinforced and challenged. As well as producing definitions of success and failure, schools, through both formal and informal relations, offer powerful interpretations of what it means to be British – of belonging and non-belonging and inclusion and exclusion. They police the boundaries of acceptable behaviour and can convey strong messages to students about who has the right to make such claims and who does not. But they also provide scope for challenging or countering these definitions – that is, there is space to challenge dominant definitions.

The strategies adopted by Asian girls, as discussed in this book, represent these spaces. They illustrate some of the ways that dominant definitions and cultural assumptions are both challenged and reinforced through formal and informal relations of schooling and the range of femininities that are (re)produced and struggled over in this process.

The **Gang girls** challenged dominant stereotypes of Asian girls as passive, timid and quiet, by becoming involved in a number of rule-breaking activities, including fighting to defend themselves from racist attack. They prioritisation of racism as a source of oppression in school led to the formation of an all-Asian female subculture, from which white students and teachers and Asian students who appeared to ally with whites in the school, were excluded.

The Gang girls were found predominantly in the lower academic sets and did not expect to study beyond compulsory schooling. In identifying racism as the main cause of their oppression, they appeared to accept and provide justification for the probability that they would not be allowed by their parents to proceed onto further education or work. They saw school as a place to have fun and adopted a number of strategies to defeat boredom, including truanting and using their home languages as a mechanism of white exclusion. They also tried to convince other Asian girls of the inevitability of their future roles solely as wives and mothers. Guiding this action was the inherent belief that change was not possible – this fatalism drew as much on their local class cultures as it did on their Asian cultures. The girls actively challenged the stereotypes of quietness and passivity but they were punished more harshly by staff for doing so than white students who similarly broke school rules. By rejecting schooling, the Gang girls played an active part in the reproduction of the conditions of their oppression.

The **Survivors** appeared to conform to the stereotypes of quiet and shy Asian girls and did not actively resist either sexism or racism in school. However, this apparent conformity was part of a conscious strategy of survival. Unlike the Gang girls, they did not use language as a mechanism for excluding white students and made a deliberate attempt to form friendships across ethnic boundaries. Although they were not exempt from name-calling, the Survivors enjoyed positive relations with white students and with staff as a result of their apparent conformity to the dominant stereotype of Asian girls.

The Survivors were in the higher academic sets in school and were determined to realise their definite career plans. The majority intended to combine a career with marriage but expected their parents to choose their marriage partners for them. Academic success was the key factor motivating their survival strategies in school and a major consequence of this response was deferred gratification. Accordingly, the girls did not involve themselves in rule-breaking activities, neither did they engage in relationships that might threaten their positive relations with parents or staff in school. They carefully secured the trust and support of their parents through their survival strategy. However, other Asian students in school labelled them as 'stuck up' because they associated with schoolmates across ethnic boundaries. Their survival strategies offer the potential to widen access into higher and further education for young Asian women but cannot be read without reference to broader patterns of discrimination that exist in the labour market.

Like the Survivors, the **Rebels** were mostly in the higher academic sets at school and enjoyed positive relations with staff. They were the most likely to dress in western fashion but as they had their parents' permission this did not indicate active resistance. Both immediate and deferred gratification was in evidence, with some of the girls allowing leisure pursuits, such as going to night-clubs, to interfere with school work. They also communicated their willingness to involve themselves in romantic relationships, but without the knowledge of parents. Their willingness to associate with members of the opposite sex and to positively dissociate with the Asian girls groups led to their experiencing sexist name-calling at school.

Although they experienced racism, the Rebels prioritised uneven gender relations within their communities. Some described their parents' views as 'backward' . Thus, on occasion their views displayed an internalisation of racist ideology and this was further evident in their negative descriptions of other young Asian women in their schools. The Rebels played an active role in the transformation of their cultures by rejecting some aspects and accepting other aspects of religious and cultural teachings. However, their actions within school were contrasted with those of other Asian girls who they characterised as 'backward' or as 'refusing to integrate'. Thus their actions unwittingly reinforced the negative imagery of Asians in British society.

Like the Gang girls, the **Faith girls** highlighted the operation of racism in school, but they did not actively involve themselves in fighting. Confrontations with other students in the school or with teachers arose only when a religious principle or practice was being attacked. The Faith girls were in the mid to higher sets and were regarded positively by staff for two main reasons: firstly, they were 'seen' to integrate, because in school they formed friendships that crossed ethnic boundaries; secondly they appeared to conform to the stereotype of the shy Asian girl.

Deferred gratification was an important consequence of this response. The Faith girls did not involve themselves actively in all-Asian friendships groups. Instead they worked conscientiously to achieve academic goals. A striking characteristic of the Faith girls was that they displayed a willingness to forsake future career plans for marriage. They were also readily accepting of their parents' choice of marriage partner. Unlike the Gang girls, this prospect did not cause them to reject schooling and replace it with strategies to defeat boredom in school. They continued to pursue academic success in the hope that their parents might allow them to succeed, so ultimately adopting a survival strategy.

A fifth strategy, of **Resistance against culture**, was not found in the main study, only in my pilot work. There were three main reasons for this, as outlined in chapter three. Firstly, most of the girls viewed their parental cultures as a positive source of identity and did not wish to resist their parents overtly. This was also the case when they required their parents' trust in order to pursue academic goals. Secondly, direct and overt resistance was not necessary for some girls, because their parents permitted them to adapt cultural practices as appropriate. Thirdly, some of the Asian girls avoided overt resistance because they had learned from the experiences of other Asian women that resistance did not pay. They knew that such resistance could have severe consequences, such as being withdrawn from school or even being 'sent back to Pakistan'. I have retained it as a possible strategy because it exists, even though it is rare.

The accounts of Asian girls presented in this book offer a challenge to fixed and static conceptions of culture. They illustrate that Asian girls, rather than being the passive recipients of fixed cultures, are actively engaged in producing new cultural identities by drawing on residual elements of their home cultures and reinterpreting them in the local cultural spaces they inhabit. These reinterpretations are shaped and influenced by a variety of factors including gender relations within their communities as well in the mainstream, their class locations and their locality. I have argued that cultures are not fixed but historically variable and that Asian girls play an active role in confirming and transforming the cultural spaces they inhabit. Therefore the strategies presented are in no way exhaustive or static and are subject to change at different historical moments and so the same young women may draw on more than one strategy at different times in their lives.

From the analysis of these girls' strategies, two main themes emerged which have practical implications for schooling. One is the need for a safe environment in which learning can take place and the other is that race and difference still have the power to shape the experiences of students but that this power can be challenged through approaches to teaching.

A safe environment for learning: dealing directly and promptly with racial incidents

Under the Race Relations (Amendment) Act 2000, all schools are now required to prepare and maintain written policies on race equality. This might take the form of policy aimed at specifically promoting 'race' equality or be contained within a broader policy approach to equal opportunities. This is an important step that emerges from the publication of the Macpherson report of 1999. However, as I argued in chapter one, these developments also need to be placed in the broader national context of educational policy that is focused on educational achievement as the solution to social exclusion and disadvantage. This means that at the same time as being asked to promote race equality, schools continue to operate within a system of marketised educational provision that has the effect of marginalising and devaluing particular groups of vulnerable students – those classified as having special needs, poor black and white working class students – who may be judged, as Gewirtz (2001) argues, as particularly 'demanding on resources and/or unlikely to be able to make a significant positive contribution to a school's examinations league-table performance'. This has an overall effect of hindering rather than promoting equality of opportunity:

> ...Students classified as belonging to those categories tend not to be selected for, and more likely to be excluded from, the schools that are most generously resourced and considered to be the most socially desirable. Hence, it would seem that the most vulnerable students are marginalised within post-welfarist contexts by being ghettoised within institutions that lack the resources to adequately serve their needs. *Inside* schools, the same groups of students are also marginalised by the increased adoption of setting practices. (Gewirtz 2001:169)

The effectiveness of race equality policies is challenged not just because of this broader policy context which places the emphasis firmly on pupils' achievements and means that inequalities are reproduced rather than exacerbated (Blair *et al.*, 1999), but also because translating written policies into action is no easy matter.

All the schools in my research study had some form of policy on race equality or equal opportunities. In many of the schools written statements were displayed in meeting rooms, some classrooms, receptions areas and staff rooms. Yet, as the accounts of the Asian girls reveal, racism and racial harassment was an accepted part of their daily school experience. A number of the girls across the eight schools also reported that they did not have confidence in the school or teachers to report such incidents. As we saw in Chapter Four, some of the Gang girls who did report such incidents found they were not believed or that no action was taken against the perpetrators.

We did see, in Chapter Six, a positive example of how racist incidents can be dealt with promptly and successfully. An Asian girl who was racially abused by a white student was supported by a member of catering staff who immediately reported the incident to the headteacher, who in turn, acted promptly to reprimand the abuser. This particular example is significant because it illustrates the importance of school space – most incidents of bullying and harassment do not take place in formal learning contexts but in playgrounds, dinner halls and outside the school gates. The fact that a member of catering staff acted so promptly indicates the school's serious commitment to stamping out racist incidents. But the incident also relied on the students having enough confidence in the school and the particular member of staff to report it in the first place. This, as we saw in Chapters four and seven, was not something that the Gang girls and some of the Faith girls felt able to do. One of the Gang girls reported, for example, an incident in which she was seriously injured by a white girl but where the teacher took no action – which led to her being further harassed. Other students also spoke of not being believed by teachers, sometimes because of her own reputation as a trouble-maker. It was this lack of confidence in school staff that encouraged those girls to seek all-Asian friendship groups, which then further endorsed the negative views some teachers had of them.

What these students most needed was to see direct and immediate *action* taken against perpetrators. For policies to be effective they need to be clearly communicated to all members of the school – management, teaching and domestic staff, assistants, anyone charged with supervision and also to the students. The fact that some girls were believed and others not reflects not only that assumptions are underpinned by broader discourses on race, but also that the power of difference is maintained and actively reproduced in schools.

Challenging the power of race and difference through teaching

We often hear the phrases 'valuing difference' or 'celebrating diversity' but their meaning is not always clear. Mahony and Hextall (2000:21) have argued that within managerialist discourse, diversity has become 'a fashionable term to replace inequality, carrying with it the clear danger of rendering invisible the structuring of social divisions and transforming them into individualised needs'. In the case of black students' schooling, the 'celebration of diversity' has sometimes been translated into a celebration of fixed and static conceptions of culture that has little relevance to the students' everyday experience.

In some approaches to teaching and learning the celebration of difference becomes an end in itself. Kundnani (2001) offers an example of this when he describes a multicultural event organised by a group of sixth-form students.

> Staff have agreed to dress up for the day in saris and kimonos and someone's dad is serving somosas out of the back of a Volvo. Workshops are

> organised on topics such as religious intolerance, ageism and racism. The phraseology of multicultural celebration is deployed avidly: the vibrancy of 'diversity', the 'tolerance of difference' ... But the mood changes in a slot that has been given over to the topic of refugees ... More than one student begins their complaints with the words, 'I'm not racist but ...' (Kundnani, 2001:41)

Without reference to, and an understanding of, the broader economic, political and social context in which the experiences of various racialised minorities in the UK have been shaped and constructed, the power relations underpinning concepts of race and difference go un-challenged. The accounts of Asian girls presented in this book also reveal the part they themselves can play in actively reproducing dominant discourses of inclusion and exclusion – the Rebels by actively dissociating themselves from the Gang girls, and the Gang girls by maintaining their separate identity.

While I have argued that internal divisions and struggles within the Asian category are important to understanding Asian girls' experiences, I do not subscribe to a view that over-focuses on these differences. Instead I see this recognition of internal struggle and division as a necessary step in challenging the broader inequalities that shape the strategies of Asian girls for coping with school in Britain. Instead of focusing on narrow differences that exist between Asian girls, the focus should be on what these racialised working class femininities have in common with other groups, especially asylum seekers, as well as minority groups in West European countries, who are also subject to racialisation processes that are shaped by historical relations of power. As the Council of Europe argues:

> Young people cannot make sense of their position and gain knowledge and mastery of it without an understanding of the international and national circumstances that shape their world. (1995:5)

With reference to schooling this means exploring not the 'who' but the 'why and how' questions of difference (Dolby, 2001). With reference to Asian girls it means moving away from fixed and static conceptions of culture to focus on how these racialised working class femininities have been shaped in a complex historical process of articulation – that is, how their lives intersect with economic, political and ideological rela-tions of subordination and domination.

Appendix I
Research Information

Table 1: Economic status of parents

	Fathers	Mothers
School A	Part -time interpreter	Adult literacy teacher
	Unemployed bus driver	Adult literacy teacher
	Engineer	Housewife
	Sales assistant	Housewife
School B	Sales assistant	Housewife
	Sales assistant	Housewife
	Work study analyst	Housewife
School C	Unemployed	Homeworker (machinist)
	Unemployed	Homeworker (machinist)
	Factory worker	Housewife
	Religious teacher	Housewife
School D	Retired ill	Housewife
	Unemployed	Housewife
	Bus driver	Homeworker (packing)
	Taxi driver	Housewife
	Taxi driver	Housewife
	Taxi driver	Housewife
	Waiter	Housewife
	Unemployed	Housewife
	Plate-maker	Homeworker (machinist)
	Factory worker (Bakery)	Homeworker
	Unemployed (former shop owner)	Unemployed (former shop owner)
School E	Unemployed	Housewife
	Taxi driver	Housewife
	Unemployed	n/a deceased
	Disabled	Housewife
	Building Contractor	Housewife
	Retired	Housewife

	Fathers	Mothers
School F	Retired	Part time-nurse
	Unemployed	Housewife
	Unemployed	Housewife
	Shop owner	Housewife
	Religious teacher	Housewife
	Unemployed	Housewife
School G	Deceased	Housewife
	Unemployed	Housewife
	Wholesaler	Housewife
	Unemployed	Unemployed
	Shop owner	Shop owner
	Unemployed	Unemployed
School H	Unemployed	Housewife
	Wholesaler	Housewife
	Unemployed	Housewife
	Unemployed	Housewife

Table 2: Schools by type and percentage of Asian students

School	Type	Gender of pupils	% Asian students
A	Comprehensive 11-16	female	20
B	Comprehensive 11-16	Mixed	68
C	Comprehensive 11-16	Mixed	24
D	Comprehensive 11-16	Mixed	19
E	Comprehensive 11-16	Mixed	10
F	Comprehensive 11-19	Mixed	47
G	Comprehensive 11-19	Mixed	33
H	Comprehensive 11-16	Mixed	65

Table 3: Interviewees by age, year of study, family religion and descent

Interviewee	Age	Year of study	Family religion	Country of origin
KP	16	11	Islam	Pakistan
YB	16	11	Islam	Pakistan
FH	16	11	Islam	Pakistan
FF	16	11	Islam	Pakistan
SR	15	11	Sikhism	India
NS	13	9	Sikhism	India
BS	14	10	Sikhism	India
SN	14	10	Islam	Pakistan
SS	13	8	Sikhism	India
PA	14	9	Islam	Pakistan
YA	13	9	Islam	Pakistan
RE	13	8	Islam	Pakistan
AS	12	8	Islam	Pakistan
AH	14	9	Islam	Pakistan
SP	14	9	Islam	Pakistan
YC	13	8	Islam	Pakistan
KB	13	8	Islam	Pakistan
NA	13	8	Islam	Pakistan
TA	13	9	Islam	Pakistan
SE	14	9	Islam	Pakistan
PD	14	9	Islam	Pakistan
RH	14	10	Islam	Pakistan
AB	15	10	Islam	Pakistan
NB	14	9	Islam	Pakistan
ST	14	10	Islam	Bangladesh
NN	14	9	Islam	Pakistan/India
AA	15	10	Islam	Pakistan
ZK	15	10	Islam	Pakistan

Interviewee	Age	Year of study	Family religion	Country of
BB	15	10	Islam	Pakistan
JB	14	10	Islam	Pakistan
NP	15	10	Islam	Pakistan
SJ	15	10	Islam	Pakistan
HB	15	10	Islam	Bangladesh
SB	15	10	Islam	Pakistan/India
TT	14	9	Islam	Pakistan
PM	14	9	Hinduism	Bangladesh
BR	13	9	Islam	Pakistan
PP	15	10	Hinduism	India
ZB	14	9	Islam	Pakistan
TH	14	10	Islam	Pakistan
NP	14	9	Islam	Pakistan
PB	14	9	Islam	Pakistan
AP	14	9	Islam	Pakistan
SL	14	9	Islam	Pakistan

Appendix 2
Resistance and Rebellion

The first young woman displayed certain characteristics of the resistance through culture model. This was evident firstly in her choice of friendships with Asian girls only: 'I don't go with the English much, I don't know, I just don't fit in with them. I'm better off with my own [Asian] friends'. Secondly, she observed that 'some teachers are nice but some are racist, they talk only to the English'. Thirdly, her attitude towards certain Asian females was judgmental:

> Some are really show-offs, you know they're always hanging with lads and they're kidding around with them thinking they're making us jealous 'cause we don't know any of them ... I don't care about the English lot, they can do what they like. It's just the Asians ... I think they should they should think about people, what they're saying like, 'look at her she's going out with lads, she's got no shame or anything'. (BB)

She did not identify racism as an obstacle in terms of choice of a future career in teaching. The only obstacle she identified was an inability to deal with children. Rather significantly however, she chose to wear western clothes secretly in defiance of her parents, for example when she went out, and at home when her parents would not see her. This was only possible because her mother, a nurse, regularly worked on night shift, and her father and sister were also often absent from the house.

> They hardly be at home, My mum is asleep. My dad is out and my sister be's at work so I have the house to myself, so I just wear English clothes then when they come home again, I wear Asian clothes again. (BB)

Although she had internalised community perceptions about girls who are seen with boys, she found it perfectly acceptable to wear skirts. She was also the only person the in the whole sample who saw herself as living with a boyfriend in ten years time, rather than being married. Despite this, she still regarded religion as important in her life, arguing, 'we can't change it now, it's part of our lives'. She did not distinguish religion from custom, stating that its greatest appeal for her concerned the extension of family ties from overseas.

For the second girl too, all Asian friendships patterns were preferred. She identified teachers as racist and she used her home language as a mechanism for excluding white people.

> We do [use language as weapon] sometimes in PE [physical education], because we know it makes the teacher mad, she can't stop us. (SN)

She did not associate with males out of classes, because her parents and brother, who attended the same school, would not allow her to. Yet she was prepared to actively resist her parents' insistence that she wore a head-scarf, removing it when she reached school. She also said that she wished to marry a person of her own choosing and could envisage an out of religion/ethnic group marriage. She complained bitterly about the Pakistani community in the area in which she lived, arguing that there was 'too much talk, I hate it'. She also declared her intention of moving away from the area as soon as she could. But she was not prepared to involve herself in a romantic relationship because 'if my dad found out, he'd send me to Pakistan'.

Bibliography

Abrams, M (1959) *The Teenage Consumer*, London, Routledge and Kegan Paul

Aggleton, P and Whitty, G (1985) 'Rebels without a cause? Socialization and sub-cultural style among the children of the new middle class', *Sociology of Education* 58:60-72

Amos, V and Parmar, P (1981) 'Resistances and responses: the experiences of black girls in Britain', in A McRobbie and T McCabe (Eds) *Feminism For Girls: an adventure story*, London, Routledge and Kegan Paul

Amos, V and Parmar, P (1984) 'Challenging imperial feminism', *Feminist Review*, (23):31-57

Angus, L (1993) The sociology of school effectiveness' *British Journal of Sociology of Education* 14(3):333-345

Anthias, F and Yuval-Davis, N (1992) *Racialized Boundaries*, London, Routledge and Kegan Paul

Anwar, M (1986) *Race and Politics: Ethnic Minorities and the British Political System*, London, Tavistock Publications

Anyon, J (1983) 'Intersections of gender and class: accommodation and resistance by working class and affluent females to contradictory sex-role ideologies', in S Walker and L Barton (Eds) *Gender, Class and Education*

Back, L (1994) 'The sounds of the city', *Anthropology in Action*, 1(1):11-16

Bains, H (1988) 'Southall youth: an old-fashioned story', in P Cohen and H Bains (Eds), *Multi-Racist Britain*

Banton, M (1997) *Racial Theories*, Cambridge, Cambridge University Press

Barker, M (1981) *The New Racism*, London, Junction Books

Barth, F (1969) *Ethnic Groups and Boundaries*, London, George Allen and Unwin

Barton, L and Walker, S (Eds) (1983) *Race, Class and Education*. London, Croom and Helm

Basit, T (1997a) *Eastern Values, Western Milieu: Identities and Aspirations of Adolescent British Muslim Girls*, Aldershot, Ashgate

Basit, T (1997b) 'I want more freedom but not too much', *Gender and Education*, 9(4):425-439

Beckerlegge, G (1991). "Strong cultures' and discrete religions: the influence of imperialism', *New Community* 17(2):201-210

Beuret, C and Makings, L (1986) 'Love in a cold climate; women, class and courtship in a recession', Paper presented to British Sociological Association Conference, Loughborough.

Bhachu, P (1991) 'Culture and ethnicity amongst Punjabi Sikh women in 1990's Britain', *New Community* 17(3):401-412

Bhattia, S (1991) 'Porn to be sold', *Tan Asian Lifestyle* 1(6):38-40

Bhavnani, K (1993) 'Towards a multicultural Europe?: "Race', nation and identity in 1992 and beyond', *Feminist Review* (45):30-45

Blackledge, D and Hunt, B (1985) *Sociological Interpretations of Education*, London, Croom Helm

Blair, M, Gillborn, D, Kemp, S and Macdonald, J (1999) 'Institutional racism, education and the Stephen Lawrence Inquiry', *Education and Social Justice* 1 (3):6-15

Brah, A (1992) 'Difference diversity and differentiation', in J Donald, and A Rattansi (Eds) *Race, Culture and Difference*, London, Sage

Brah, A (1993) 'Reframing Europe: en-gendered racisms, ethnicities and nationalisms in contemporary Western Europe', *Feminist Review* (43):9-28

Brah, A (1994) 'Time, place and others: discourses of race, nation and ethnicity', *Sociology* 28(3):805-13

Brah, A(1996) *Cartogrophies of Diaspora*, London, Routledge

Brah, A and Minhas, R (1985) 'Structural racism or cultural difference', in G Weiner (Ed) *Just a Bunch of Girls*

Cain, M (1986) 'Realism, feminism, methodology and the law', *International Journal of Sociology of Law*, 14(3-4):255-267

Campbell, A (1984) *Girls in the Gang*, New York, Basil Blackwell

Cambell, H (1980) 'Rasatafari – culture of resistance', *Race and Class* xxii(1):1-23

Carby, H (1982) 'Schooling in Babylon', in Centre for Contemporary Cultural Studies *The Empire Strikes Back*

Carby, H (1982) 'White woman listen! Black feminism and the boundaries of sisterhood', in Centre for Contemporary Cultural Studies *The Empire Strikes Back*

Campaign Against Racism and Fascism (CARF) (1991) '1981-1991: How racist is Britain?', *CARF* 3 (June/August):8-11

Campaign Against Racism and Fascism (CARF) (1992) 'Racist murders', *CARF* 11 (November/ December):10

Campaign Against Racism and Fascism (CARF) (1993) 'Racist attacks, more deaths', *CARF* 14 (May/June):12

Campaign Against Racism and Fascism (CARF) (2001) 'The summer of rebellion': *CARF* Special Report, CARF 63 London, CARF at http://www.carf.demon.co.uk/feat54.html

Campaign Against Racism and Fascism (CARF) (2002) 'Community Cohesion: Blunkett's new race doctrine', *CARF* 67, London, CARF at http://www.carf.demon.co.uk/feat56.html

Carter, H (2001) Riot trigger attack on pensioner was not racial', *Guardian Unlimited*, Thursday September 20 at http://www.guardian.co.uk/racism/Story/0,2763,554719,00.html

Cashmore, E (1979) *Rastaman: The Rastafarian Movement in England*, London, George Allen and Unwin

Cashmore, E and Troyna, B (Eds) (1982) *Black Youth in Crisis*, London, George Allen and Unwin

Cashmore, E and Troyna, B (1990) *Introduction to Race Relations*, London, Falmer Press

Central Statistical Office (1993) *Social Trends, 23*, London, HMSO

Centre for Contemporary Cultural Studies (1982) *The Empire Strikes Back*, London, Hutchinson

Cohen, P and Bains, H (Eds) (1988) *Multiracist Britain*, London, Macmillan

Coleman, J (1962) *The Adolescent Society*, New York, Free Press

Commission for Racial Equality (1994) *Annual Report*, London, CRE

Commission for Racial Equality (1999a) *Ethnic Minorities in Britain*, London, CRE

Commission for Racial Equality (1999b) Racial incidents reported to the Police in England, Wales and Scotland, 1997/8,

Commission for Racial Equality (2002) *Annual Report*, London, CRE

Community Relations Commission (CRC) (1976) *Between Two Cultures*, CRC

Connolly, C (1991) 'Washing our linen: one year of Women Against Fundamentalism'. *Feminist Review* 37:68-77

Connolly, P (1998) *Racism, Gender Identities and Schooling*, London, Routledge

Council of Europe (1995) *All Different, All Equal*, Education Pack, Strasbourg, European Youth Centre

Corrigan, P (1976) 'Doing nothing', in S Hall and T Jefferson (Eds) *Resistance Through Rituals*, London, Hutchinson

Cotsgrove and Parker (1963) 'Work and non work', *New Society*, July

Davies, B and Harre, R (1991) 'Positioning: the discursive production of selves', *Journal for the Theory of Behaviour*, 20(1): 44-63

Deakin, N (1970) *Colour, Citizenship and British Society*, London, Panther Books

Department of Employment (1993) 'Ethnic origins in the labour market' *Employment Gazette* (February): 25-43

Department for Education and Employment (DfEE) (1997) *Excellence in Schools*, London, The Stationery Office

Department for Education and Skills (DfES) (2001) *Schools Building on Success: Raising Standards, Promoting Diversity, Achieving Results*, London, The Stationery Office

Derrida, J (1978) *Writing and Difference*, London, Routledge and Kegan Paul

Dews, P (1987) *Logics of Disintegration*, London, Verso

Dex, S (1987) *Women's Occupational Mobility*, London, Macmillan

Diamond I and Quinby, L (1988) (Eds) *Feminism and Foucault: Reflections on Resistance* Boston, Northeastern University Press

Dodd D (1978) 'Police and thieves on the streets of Brixton', *New Society*, 16 March

Dolby, N (2001) *Constructing Race: Youth, Identity and Popular Culture in South Africa*, New York, State University of New York Press

Donald, J and Rattansi, A (1992) (Eds) *'Race', Culture and Difference*, London, Sage

Downes, D (1966) *The Delinquent Solution*, London, Routledge, Kegan Paul

Drury, B M (1991) 'Sikh girls and the maintenance of an ethnic culture', *New Community* 17(3): 387-399

Epstein, D and Johnson, R (1998) *Schooling Sexualities*, Buckingham, Open University Press

Forgacs, D (1988) *A Gramsci Reader*, London, Lawrence and Wishart

Fryer, P (1985) *Staying Power: The History of Black People in Britain*, London, Pluto Press

Fryer, P (1988) *Black People in the British Empire: An Introduction*, London, Pluto

Fuller, M (1980) 'Black girls in a London comprehensive school', in R Deem (Ed) *Schooling For Women's Work*, Routledge and Kegan Paul

Fuller, M (1982) 'Young female and black', in B Troyna and R Hatcher, *Black Youth in Crisis*, London, George Allen and Unwin

Fuller, M (1983) 'Qualified criticism, critical qualifications', in L Barton and S Walker (Eds) *Race, Class and Education*

Garland, D (1996) 'The limits of the sovereign state: strategies of crime control in contemporary society', *British Journal of Criminology*, 36(4):445-471

Gewirtz, D (1991) 'Analyses of racism and sexism in education and strategies for change', *British Journal of Sociology of Education*, 12 (2):183-201

Gewirtz, S (1998) 'Post-welfarist schooling: a social justice audit' *Education and Social Justice* 1(1):52-64

Gewirtz, S (2001) *The Managerial School: Post-welfarism and Social Justice in Education,* London, Routledge

Gill D, Mayor B, and Blair M (1992) *Racism and Education*, London, Sage

Gillborn, D (1997) 'Young, black and failed by school: the market, education reform and black students, *Journal of Inclusive Education*, 1(1):65-87

Gillborn, D and Gipps, C (1996) *Recent Research on the Achievements of Ethnic Minority Pupils.* Ofsted Reviews of Research. London, Ofsted

Gilroy, P (1982) Police and thieves, in Centre for Contemporary Cultural Studies *The Empire Strikes Back*

Gilroy, P (1987) *Ain't No Black in the Union Jack: The Cultural Politics of Race and Nation,* London, Hutchinson

Gilroy, P and Lawrence, E (1988) 'Two-tone Britain: white and black youth and the politics of anti-racism', in P Cohen and H Bains (Eds), *Multi-Racist Britain*

Giroux, H (1983) 'Ideology, agency and the process of schooling', in L Barton and S Walker (Eds) *Social Crisis and Educational Research,* London, Croom Helm

Goldberg, D (1990) *Anatomy of Racism,* Minneapolis, University of Minnesota Press

Gramsci, A (1971) *The Prison Notebooks*, London, Lawrence and Wishart

Grant, L (1993) 'Miss Asia looses culture clash', *Independent on Sunday* 14 February

Griffin, C (1985) *Typical Girls? Young Women from School to the Job Market,* London, Routledge Kegan and Paul

Griffin, C (1986) Black and white youth in a declining job market: unemployment amongst Asian, Afro Caribbean and White young people in Leicester, Centre For Mass Communications Research, Leicester University Research Report Series

Griffin, C (1993) *Representations of Youth*, Cambridge, Polity Press

Gutzmore, C (1983) 'Capital, "Black youth" and crime', *Race and Class* xxv(2):13-30

Hall, S (1980) 'Race, articulation and societies structured in dominance', in *Sociological Trends: Race and Colonialism*, Paris, UNESCO

Hall, S (1988) *The Hard Road to Renewal: Thatcherism and the Crisis of the Left*, London, Verso

Hall, S (1990) 'Cultural, Identity and Diaspora' in J Rutherford (Ed) *Identity, Culture, Community, Difference*

Hall, S (1992) 'New ethnicities', in J Donald and A Rattansi (Eds), *Race, Culture, Difference*

Hall, S, Critcher, C Jefferson, T, Clark, J and Roberts, B (1978) *Policing the Crisis: Mugging, the State and Law and Order*, London, Macmillan

Hall, S and Jefferson, T (Eds) (1975) *Resistance Through Rituals*, London, Hutchinson

Halston, J (1989) 'The sexual harassment of young women', in Holly, L (Ed) *Girls and Sexuality: Teaching and Learning,* Milton Keynes, Open University Press

Hargreaves, A (1982) 'Resistance and relative autonomy theories: problems of distortion and incoherence in recent Marxist analyses of education', *British Journal of Sociology of Education* 3(2):107-126

Hargreaves, J (1990) 'Urban dance-styles and self-identities: The specific case of Bhangra', *Sport: Kultur Veranderung* (19):146-160

Harris, P (2001) 'Fears of racial time-bomb in riot-hit towns', *Guardian Unlimited* Sunday August 5 at http://www.guardian.co.uk/racism/Story/0,2763,53249,00.html

Haw, K (11994) 'Muslim girls' schools: a conflict of interests?' *Gender and Education*, 6(1):63-76

Haynes, F (1992) *Marching on Together: A Reappraisal of Leeds, the Lads and the Meeja*, Manchester Polytechnic Unit for Law and Popular Culture, Working Paper

Heidensohn, F (1985) *Women and Crime*, London, Macmillan

Home Office (1996) *Taking Steps, The Third Report of the Racial Attacks Group*, London, The Stationery Office

Home Office (2001) *Community Cohesion: A Report of Independent Review Team led by Ted Cantle*, London, The Stationery Office

Kabbani, R (1989) *Letter to Christendom*, London, Virago

Kenny, A (1999) 'What happened to antiracist education?' *Education and Social Justice* 1(3): 2-4

Kerr, M (1958) *The People of Ship Street*, London, Routledge and Kegan Paul

Khan, V S (1977) 'The Pakistanis', in J L Watson (Ed) *Between Two Cultures*, Oxford, Basil Blackwell

Khan, V S (1976) 'Pakistani women in Britain', *New Community*, 5 (1-2):99-108

Khanum, S (1991) 'Naked ambition', *New Statesman and Society* 4 (175):12-13

Klug, F (1989) 'Oh to be in England: the British case study', in F Anthias and N Yuval Davis (Eds), *Woman Nation State*, London, Macmillan

Knight, I (1993) 'Why this Asian babe is browned off', *Guardian* 4 October

Knott, K and Khoker, S (1993) 'Religious and ethnic identity among young Muslim women in Bradford', *New Community* 19(4):593-610

Kundnani, K (2001) 'In a Foreign land: the new popular racism', *Race and Class* 43(2):41-60

Lawrence, E (1982) 'Just plain common sense: the roots of racism', in Centre for Contemporary Cultural Studies, *The Empire Strikes Back*

Layton-Henry, Z (1992) *The Politics of Immigration*, Oxford, Blackwell

Lees S (1997) *Ruling Passions: Sexual Violence, Reputation and the Law*, Buckingham, Open University Press

Leonard, E (1987) *Women, Crime and Society*, London, Longman

Lowman, J (1989) *Street Prostitution. Assessing the Impact of the Law*, Vancouver, Ottawa, Department of Justice

Mac an Ghaill, M (1988) *Young, Gifted and Black: Student-Teacher Relations in the Schooling of Black Youth*, Milton Keynes, Open University Press

Mac an Ghaill, M (1992) 'Coming of age in the 1980's England: reconceptualising black students' schooling experience, in D Gill et al (Eds), *Racism and Education*

Mac an Ghaill (1994) *The Making of Men*, Buckingham, Open University Press

Macpherson, W, *et al* (1999) *The Stephen Lawrence Inquiry*, London, The Stationery Office

McRobbie, A and Garber, J (1975) 'Girls and subcultures', in S Hall and T Jefferson (Eds), *Resistance Through Rituals: Youth Subcultures in Post-war Britain*

MacRobbie, A (1991) *Feminism and Youth Culture: From Jackie to Just Seventeen*, London, Macmillan

Mahony, P and Hextall, I (2000) *Reconstructing Teaching: Standards, Performance and Accountability,* London, RoutledgeFalmer

Malik, K (1989) 'The Rushdie affair: The 'sleeping demons' awake', in *Living Marxism*, (May):24-27

Mani, L and Frankenburg, R (1993) 'Cross currents, crosstalk: race, 'postcoloniality' and the politics of location', *Cultural Studies*, 7(2):292-400

Mays, J (1954) *Juvenile Delinquency,* London, Jonathan Cape

Mercer, K (1990) 'Welcome to the jungle: identity and diversity in postmodern politics', in J Rutherford (Ed), *Identity, Community, Culture, Difference*

Miles, R (1982) *Racism and Migrant Labour*, London, Routledge and Kegan Paul

Miles, R (1984) 'Marxism versus the sociology of race relations', *Ethnic and Racial Studies* 7(2): 217-37

Miles, R (1989) *Racism,* London, Routledge

Miles, R (1993) *Racism After race Relations*, London, Routledge

Mirza, H S (1992) *Young, Female and Black*, London, Routledge

Mirza, K (1989) 'The silent cry: second generation Bradford Muslim women speak', *Muslims in Europe* 43, Centre for the study of Islam and Christian-Muslim Relations

Modood, T (1988) 'Black racial equality and Asian identity', *New Community* 12(3):397-404

Modood, T. (1992) 'British Asian Muslims and the Rushdie affair', in J. Donald and A Rattansi (Eds) *Race, Culture, Difference*

Mulhern, F (2000) *Culture/Metaculture*, London, Routledge

National Statistics Office (NSO) (2002) *Social Trends* 32, London, NSO

Norris, S and Read, E (1985) *Out in the Open: People talking About Being Gay or Bisexual,* London, Pan

Office of Population and Census Surveys (OPCS) (1993) *The Labour Force Survey*, London, OPCS

Office for Standards in Education (Ofsted) (1999) *Raising the Attainment of Minority Ethnic Pupils: School and LEA Responses*, London, Ofsted

Open University (1993) The burden of representation, Course Ed, 386, *Race, Education and Society,* Milton Keynes, Open University

Phillips and Brown (1998) *Entry into the Criminal Justice System: A Survey of Police Arrests and Their Outcomes,* Home Office Research Study 185

Ozga, J (1999) 'Two nations? education and social inclusion-exclusion in Scotland and England', *Education and Social Justice* 1 (3): 44-50

Parker-Jenkins, M (1994) 'Islam shows its diverse identities', *Times Educational Supplement* 21 October

Parmar, P (1984) 'Hateful contraries', *Ten* 8, (16):71-78

Parmar, P (1988) 'Gender, race and power: The Challenge to Youth Work Practice', in P Cohen and H Bains (Eds), *Multiracist Britain*

Parmar, P (1990) 'Black feminism and the politics of articulation', in J Rutherford (Ed) *Identity, Community, Culture, Difference*

Parmar, P and Mirza, N (1983) 'Steppin' forward – working with Asian young women' *Gen* (1):16-19

Pugh, R (1991) 'Culture clash on their plate', *Times Educational Supplement* 8 March

Race Today Collective (1983) *The Struggle of Asian Workers in Britain*, London, Blackrose.

Raphael, A (1994) 'Not just an Asian babe', *Guardian*, 1 August

Rashid, S (1981) The socialisation and education of Pakistani teenage girls in London. Unpublished Mphil thesis, London: School of Oriental and African Studies

Redhead, S (1991) *Football with Attitude*, Manchester, Wordsmith

Rex, J (1970) *Race Relations in Sociological Theory*, London, Weidenfield and Nicolson

Rex, J and Tomlinson, S (1979) *Colonial Immigrants in a British City,* London, Routledge and Kegan Paul

Riley, K (1985) 'Black girls speak for themselves', in G Weiner (Ed) *Just a Bunch of Girls*

Roberts, N (1986) *Frontline: Women in the Sex Industry Speak*, London, Grafton Books.

Roman, L (1988) 'Intimacy, labour and class: ideologies of feminine sexuality in the punk slam dance', in L Roman and L Christian-Smith (Eds), *Becoming Feminine*

Roman, L and Christian-Smith, L (Eds) (1988) *Becoming Feminine: The Politics of Popular Culture*, New York, Taylor and Francis

Rose, E J B, Deakin, N, Abrahams, M, Jackson, V, Preston, M, Vanags, A H, Cohen, B, Gaitskill, J and Ward P (1969) *Colour and Citizenship*, London, Oxford University Press for the Institute of Race Relations

Runnymede Trust (1993) 'Growing gap between ethnic minority groups', *Runnymede Trust Bulletin* (265):4-5

Russel, S (1993) 'The Empire Strikes Back', *Sunday Times* 4 October

Rutherford, J (Ed) (1990) *Identity, Community, Culture, Difference*, London, Lawrence and Wishart

Saghal, G and Yuval-Davis, N (1992) *Refusing Holy Orders,* London, Virago

Samad, Y and Eade, J (2002) *Community Perceptions of Forced Marriages*, Community Liason Unit, Foreign and Commonwealth Office

Samad, Y (1992) 'Book burning and race relations: political mobilisation of Bradford Muslims', *New Community* 18(4):507-19

Searle, C (1993) 'Race before wicket, empire and the white rose', *Race and Class* 31(3):31-48

Sewell, T (1998) *Black Masculinities and Schooling: How Black Boys Survive Modern Schooling* Stoke-on-Trent, Trentham Books

Shah, R (1992) *The Silent Minority: Children With Disabilities in Asian Families*, National Children's Bureau

Shain, F (1996) A Study of the experiences and responses of Asian girls in secondary education in Britain. Unpublished PhD thesis, Keele University

Sharp, S (1976) *Just Like a Girl: How Girls Learn to be Women*, Harmondsworth, Penguin

Shaw, A (1988) *A Pakistani Community in Britain*, Oxford, Basil Blackwell

Siddiqui, H (1991) 'Winning freedoms', *Feminist Review* 37:18-20

Singh, R (1991) 'Ethnic minority experience in Higher Education', *Higher Education Quarterly* (44):344-58

Sivanandan, A (1982) *A Different Hunger*, London, Pluto Press

Sivanandan, A (1983) 'From resistance to rebellion: Asian and Afro-Caribbean struggles in Britain', *Race and Class* 23 (2\3):111-52

Sivanandan, A (2000) 'UK: reclaiming the struggle' *Race and Class* 42(2):67-73

Smart, C (1976) *Women, Crime and Criminology*, London, Routledge and Kegan Paul

Solomos, J (1992) 'The politics of immigration since 1945', in P Braham, A Rattansi, and R Skellington (Eds), *Racism and Anti Racism*, London, Sage

Solomos, J and Back, L (1994) 'Conceptualising racisms: social theory, politics and research', *Sociology* 28(1):143-161

Southall Black Sisters (1990) *Against the Grain: A Celebration of Survival and Struggle*, London, Southall Black Sisters

Spinley, M (1953) *The Deprived and the Privelaged*, London, Routledge and Kegan Paul

Sprott W J, Jephcott, P and Carter, M (1954) *The Social Background of Delinquency*, Nottingham, University of Nottingham Press

Taylor, M (1985) *The Best of Both Worlds*, Oxford, NFER

Tomlinson, S (1983) 'Black women in higher education – case studies of university women in Britain' in L Barton and S Walker (Eds), *Race, Class and Education*

Troyna, B (1987) (Ed) *Racial Inequality in Education*, London, Tavistock

Ullah, P (1985) 'Disaffected black and white youth: the role of unemployment duration and perceived job discrimination', *Ethnic and Racial Studies* 8:181-93

Walker, D (2002) 'Study reveals jobs plight of Muslims', *Guardian Unlimited* Politics at http://politics.guardian.co.uk/homeaffairs/story/0,11026,652990,00.html

Walker, S and Barton, L (Eds) *Gender, Class and Education*, Lewes, Falmer Press

Ware, V (1992) *Beyond the Pale: White Women, Racism and History*, London, Verso.

Watson, J (1977) (Ed) *Between Two Cultures: Migrants and Minorities in Britain*, Oxford, Basil Blackwell

Weiner, G (1985) (Ed) *Just A Bunch of Girls*, Milton Keynes, Open University Press

Whitty, G (1998) 'New labour, education and disadvantage', *Education and Social Justice* 1 (1):2-8

Wilce, H (1984) 'Walking the tightrope between two cultures', *Times Educational Supplement* 10 February

Williams, R (1980) 'Base and superstructure in Marxist cultural theory' in R. Williams *Problems in Materialism and Culture*, London, New Left Books

Willis, P (1977) *Learning to Labour: How Working Class Kids Get Working Class Jobs*, Saxon House

Willis, P (1990) *Common Culture*, Milton Keynes, Open University Press

Wilson , A (1984) *Finding a Voice: Asian Women in Britain*, London, Virago

WING (1985) *Women, Immigration and Nationality Group: Worlds Apart, Women Under Immigration Law*, London, Pluto Press

Wise, S (1995) 'Why Asian women still run away from home', *Cosmopolitan* (March):12-15

Woods, P and Hammersley, M (Eds) (1994) *Gender and Ethnicity in Schools: Ethnographic Accounts*, London, Routledge

Women Against Fundamentalism (WAF) (1991) *Newsletter No.1.*

Wright, C (1987). 'The relations between teachers and Afro-Caribbean pupils: Observing Multi-cultural Classrooms', in G. Weiner (Ed) *Gender Under Scrutiny New Inquiries in Education*, London, Hutchinson

Wright, C (1992) 'Early education: multiracial primary school classrooms', in D Gill et al (Eds) Racism and Education

Wright, C (1994) 'School processes: an ethnographic study', in P Woods and M Hammersley (Eds), *Gender and Ethnicity in Schools* http://www.cre.gov.uk/duty/index.html

Index

fatalism 45, 76, 126
feminist
 – analyses 29
 – literature 49
 – research 30
friendships 67-69, 80-81, 87, 88, 97, 108, 113, 119, 120, 126
fundamentalist ix, 141
future aspirations/prospects 65-67, 72-73, 76, 90-91, 100, 107-108,116-117, 123, 124, 126, 128

Gang girls 56, 57, 59-76, 77, 79, 82, 86, 91, 96, 97, 98, 100, 101, 102, 103, 107, 113, 114, 117, 121, 126, 128, 129, 130, 132
gender discrimination 84, 91, 92, 100, 127
gender relations 93
global 13, 14, 38
globalisation 38
Gramsci 36-38, 42, 43, 44, 85
Gulf War ix, 21, 88

hegemony 36-37, 44, 68, 76
hijab vii, 96, 118-119
Hindu
 – community 7
 – cultures 8
 – girls 54
Hindus 10, 13, 13, 41, 89, 90, 106, 111
historical specificity 36, 38

immediate gratification 127
immigration 38-39
imperialism 32, 38
inner city disturbances vii, x, 12, 14, 17, 40, 73, 125
integrate
 – refusal to 96, 98, 109, 125, 128
 – willingness to 91, 109, 128
 – seen to 120, 128
 – failure to vii
integration vii, ix, 73, 97
language viii, viii, 8, 10, 15, 22, 33, 41, 65, 82-83, 97-98, 119-120

Macpherson 12, ff27, 129
marriage 4, 73, 80, 90, 91, 105, 107, 108, 117, 127, 128
 – arranged 3, 7, 9, 41, 86, 112, 123
 – forced viii, 3, 6, 9, 73, 123
 – love 72
masculinities
 – Asian 25,40, 60, 74
 – in schooling 40
mothers viii, 5
Muslim
 – fundamentalism 52, 125
 – girls 53, 54, 71, 95, 97, 99, 116, 123
 – communities viii, 26
 – cultures 8
Muslims vii, 10, 13, 15, 17, 18, 20, 21, 22, 23, 25, 26, 34, 35, 41, 71, 72, 78, 88, 90, 98, 102, 105, 106, 107, 111, 112, 120, 122, 125

name-calling
 – racist 59-61, 80, 82, 87-89, 93, 94, 101-103, 122, 127
 – sexist 80-81, 103-104, 127

positioning ix, 8, 41, 42, 59, 88
punishment 75, 126

Race Relations Amendment Act (2000) 129
racism vii, 1, 5, 7, 11-15, 32, 34,35, 47, 50, 77, 78, 79, 81, 93, 94, 100, 101, 103, 112, 115, 126, 127, 130
 – and education policy 13-15
 – criminal justice 11-13
 – definition of 1, ff27
 – denial of 56, 128
 – institutional ff27, 32, 112, 115, 116
racial attack 11, 13, 75, 126
racial discrimination 48, 92, 96, 116

racial harassment *see also* name-calling 11, 12, 33, 80, 81, 82, 87, 93, 100, 101-102, 103, 122, 127
racial tension 19, 25, 60
racial violence 24, 60-61, 78
racialisation of immigration 1,2, 15-17, 40
racialised discourses 2-14, 15, 26, 40, 98, 104, 113, 114
racially motivated crime 11
rebel 81, 91
'rebellion' *see* Rebels, 127-128, 137-138
Rebels 56, 57, 93-109, 127-128
religion 71-72, 89-90, 105-107, 111, 113, 123, 124
religious prioritisation 56 *see also* Faith girls
resistance 29, 33, 34, 42, 43,45, 48, 51, 60, 82, 83, 89, 103, 118, 126, 128, 137-138
resistance against culture 56, 104, 117
resistance strategies *see also* cultures of resistance 43-48, 46, 49-53, 51, 54
'resistance through culture' 55, 56 *see also* Gang girls
'riots' vii, 15, 40 *see also* inner city disturbances
Rushdie ix, 17-21, 22, 40, 88

September 11 viii, x, 26, 40, 88, 125
sexuality
 – as a social division 42
 – heterosexuality 1, 2-3, 9,27, 87, 103
 – homosexuality 5, 9, ff27
 – policing of 52, 69-70
 – sexual availability 40
 – sexual freedom 25
 – school culture 59
 – writing on 31
sexism 5, 77, 101, 116, 126
sexist labelling 69-70, 80-81, 103-104, 127
sexual discrimination *see also* gender